AF334182

OVERBOARD!

A Provocative History of the
U.S.S. J.P. Kennedy, Jr. (DD-850)

By Claire Branand

<u>*Editor's Note*</u>:

The following document is based on a true story. The names have not been changed, except for the name of the Author's roommate in order to protect her privacy. [See *U.S.S. J.P. Kennedy, Jr.* Deck Log attached]. The Author, Claire Branand, née: Dostal, was the Plaintiff in the lawsuit.

All rights and use of this manuscript are reserved. No part of this manuscript may be reproduced or transmitted in any form or by any means, electronic or mechanical, including photocopying, recording, or by any information storage and retrieval system, without permission in writing from the author.

Copyright © 1997, Claire D. Branand
All rights reserved

Library of Congress Cataloguing-in-Publication Data:

Branand, Claire D.

    OVERBOARD!
    Historical Account

    ISBN 0-9675160-0-5

    Published by:
    Skye Publishing
    P.O. Box 4562
    Annapolis, MD 21403

Cover photo courtesy of the U.S. Naval Institute

PREFACE

The Navy is a branch of the armed forces of the United States. Its mission is to help protect and defend the right of the United States and our allies to move freely on the oceans and to protect our country against enemies.

To accomplish these tasks, the Navy has nearly 500,000 men and women serving on more than 400 ships and submarines, 1,000 aircraft and shore bases around the world.

Aircraft carriers form the core of our Navy's surface forces. The *Nimitz*-class aircraft carrier is the largest warship in the world, weighing more than 90,000 tons, with a 4.5-acre flight deck, a crew of nearly 6,000, and about 100 aircraft of various types that perform many different combat missions.

The Navy also has dozens of other surface ships such as cruisers, destroyers, frigates, tenders and auxiliary ships.

The submarine force consists of attack submarines (SSNs) and ballistic missile submarines (SSBNs).

A vital mission of the nuclear attack submarine is to protect our fleet by finding and tracking enemy ships and submarines, and if necessary, attacking them with its high-speed torpedoes and missiles.

Ballistic missile submarines are part of America's nuclear deterrent force. They patrol beneath the oceans of the world carrying long-range, nuclear-warhead missiles.

All modern submarines are quiet and comfortable. While a submarine patrols hundreds of feet below the surface, the air temperature and humidity are scientifically controlled for complete comfort. Submarines carry crews of 110 to 140 enlisted men and 12 to 14 officers. Nuclear powered submarines and surface ships can operate for 10 to 15 years without refueling.

The Navy also has a large naval air force with about 4,000 aircraft such as fighter planes, helicopters and patrol aircraft.

These planes are truly impressive. The F/A-18 *Hornet*, for example, can intercept and attack enemy targets in the air and on the ground with a wide variety of weapons.

Navy aircraft are based at sea on aircraft carriers and ashore at naval air stations. Missions can include everything from air defense for the fleet to civilian disaster relief.

All these naval forces combined—surface, submarine, air and land—allow the Navy to effectively do its job. The Navy represents teamwork at its best.

CONTENTS

PART ONE: *The U.S.S. J.P. Kennedy, Jr.*
- I.   America's Cup Races
- II.   Guantanamo Bay
- III.   Cruising
- IV.   The Gemini Space Probe

PART TWO: *Newport Naval Base*
- V.   The Fall
- VI.   The Rescue
- VII.   Naval Base Hospital
- VIII.   The Escort

PART THREE: *In Boston*
- IX.   The Rape
- X.   United States v. Short
- XI.   The Investigator
- XII.   Going Home

PART FOUR: *Dostal vs. The United States of America*
- XIII.   The Complaint
- XIV.   Interrogatories
- XV.   Discovery of Documents
- XVI.   History of the Kennedy

PART FIVE: *The Silence*
          XVII.   The Kennedy 1965-1972
          XVIII.   The Freedom of Information Act
          XIX.   Retrieving the Files
          XX.   Women and the Military

PART SIX: *The Conclusion*
          XXI.   The Pre-Trial Memorandum
          XXII.   The Settlement
          XXIII.   Sources

PART ONE:

The U.S.S. J.P. Kennedy, Jr.

I. <u>*America's Cup Races*</u>

The 66 foot *Weatherly*, which was designed by Phil Rhodes, arrived in Newport from the New York City Yacht Club in the misty chill of Spring, 1962. She was to compete with the 69 foot *Gretel* in that year's America's Cup race.

The challenge was held on the unforgiving Narragansett Bay near the Newport Naval Base. President John F. Kennedy was the honored guest on board the destroyer, the *U.S.S. J.P. Kennedy, Jr.*, along with his family and the Secret Service, to watch this exhilarating race.

The *Weatherly*'s challenger, the *Gretel*, had been designed by Alan Payne. Sir Frank Packer & Syndicate owned this distinguished yacht which hailed from Sydney, Australia.

In 1956, the New York Yacht Club petitioned and later gained agreement from the New York State Court to change the Deed of Gift to lessen the permitted waterline length to 44 feet, which then allowed the smaller 12-meter boats to race in the America's Cup. Another advantage of the altered deed which concerned the passage of challenging boats to the race course, was that it now allowed countries from all over the world to compete. In the past, the rules stated that a Challenging Yacht Club had to be within sailing distance of Rhode Island.[1]

Australia participated in the race for the first time in 1962. Sir Frank Packer, a newspaper magnate, made that dare. By using his great fortunes, he built the *Gretel* and chartered the *Vim*, as a trial horse. The

---

[1] The *Sail Magazine Book of Sailing*, by Peter Johnson.

New York City Yacht Club felt that the depth of 12-meter knowledge in Australia was limited, so an older boat, the *Weatherly*, was entered by the U.S. It soon became apparent that the "wrong boat" had been chosen. Although she defeated the *Gretel* by 4 races to 1, the winning margins were very close. The 26 second victory in the 5th race was, indeed, by "a nose".

On board the *Kennedy*, little John-John was decked out in a miniature sailor's suit. He spent most of the day saluting sailors, while his sister, Caroline, was shown a demonstration by a signalman (Semaphore via flags). This same signalman would later witness the horror of a woman falling off the *Kennedy* after slamming into the side of the *Forrest Sherman*, which was berthed next to the *Kennedy* the following year, in Newport.

As the *Weatherly* rounded the final mark in the race, closely trailed by the *Gretel*, a huge applause broke out on the *Kennedy* as everyone cheered the American win. Commander Mikhalevsky saluted the American flag, while the Navy's Chorus sang the National Anthem.

After rounding the final mark behind *Weatherly* (left), the *Gretel* was quicker hoisting its spinnaker and surfed past to win in the second race in 1962. Photo courtesy of Rosenfeld Collection, Mystic Seaport Museum.

II.   *Guantanamo Bay*

During the Cuban Missile Crisis, the United States sent Polaris Submarines and the *U.S.S. J.P. Kennedy, Jr.* and the *U.S.S. Pierce* to Guantanamo Bay in Cuba. On October 26, 1962, shortly after the America's Cup Race, the two destroyers carried out the first interception of the Cuban Crisis by halting and boarding the Russian chartered freighter, *MARULCA* in mid-October.

The United States' Strategic Air Command launched American U-2 reconnaissance planes to photograph missile sites that were being constructed near San Cristobel. During that time, Russia had provided Cuba with thousands of technicians and soldiers, along with around 40 of the latest MIG-21 fighter-bombers, and unassembled Ilyushin-28 bombers, tanks, artillery, SAM missiles, and antiaircraft guns.

Spokesmen for President Kennedy described the Soviet build-up in Cuba as defensive. When President Kennedy reviewed the findings of the U-2 mission, he addressed the public on television on October 22, stating that the Russian military installations were offensive. If the U-2 mission had been postponed for 9-10 days, the Soviet missile would have been operational by then.

Kennedy advised the military to read everything that had been written by Mao Zedong and Castro's military advisor, Ché Guevara, about guerrilla warfare.[2]

The Soviet missiles (IRBMs), when equipped with warheads, were tough enough to raze U.S. military bases and were capable of slaying millions of Americans.

During President Kennedy's Address to the Nation on October 22, he stated that "Our unswerving objective must be to prevent the use of these missiles

---

[2]Schlesinger.

Aerial recon taken by the C.I.A. during the Cuban Crisis, 1962. Courtesy U.S.N.I.

U.S.S. J.P. Kennedy, Jr (DD 850)
crewmen board Russian-leased, Lebanese
freighter Marulca during the Cuban
Missile Crisis, 1962 - Courtesy U.S.N.I.

El Morro Castle, Havana, Cuba, photographed from a U.S. Navy airplane. From the collection of VAdm. Dixwell Ketcham.

Missile Disarmament in the 60's
Source: U.S. Naval Institute

A U.S. Marine stands guard at Guantanamo Bay, Cuba.
Courtesy U.S.N.I.

U.S. soldiers based at Guantanamo Bay, Cuba -
Courtesy U.S.N.I.

Mine Sweepers and Radar Picket ships
at Guantanamo Bay, Cuba - Courtesy U.S.N.I.

against this or any other country and to secure their withdrawal or elimination from the Western Hemisphere."[3]

As the crewmen aboard the *U.S.S. J.P. Kennedy, Jr.* left Porto Caimanera in Guantanamo Bay, they viewed the sheltered 8-mile inlet where the United States Naval Base stood on 28,000 acres, with its airfields and extensive supply, repair and training facilities.

That late Summer and Fall of 1962 were traumatic times for the crew of the *Kennedy*. The ship did not log in any further outstanding events until May 3, 1963.

FOR OFFICIAL USE ONLY   DECK LOG—SMOOTH REMARKS SHEET
NAVPERS-711 (New 10-14)

UNITED STATES SHIP JOSEPH P. KENNEDY, JR. (DD 850)   Friday, 3 May 19 63
(Day) (Date) (Month)

SMOOTH REMARKS—CONTINUED

16–20   Moored as before. 1625 Let fires die under #3 boiler. 1705 Commenced taking on fuel. 1725 Secured from taking on fuel. 1811 Miss Claire Dostal fell overboard at the quarterdeck, port side, amidships between this ship and the SHERMAN. Man overboard was passed on all circuits. Rescue was being performed by the Quarterdeck Watch VANDERHOUDE, IC1. BRINGHURST, SH3 and COSTA, SN when OOD arrived on the scene. 1815 Miss Dostal was recovered from the water and sent to sick bay for check-up by PALADACHUCK, HM1 who found no apparent injuries. She was given the privacy of sickbay with a friend, Miss Ruth A. Green while her clothes were being dried. 1905 Miss Dostal was sent by ambulance under the custody of PITTS, HMSN to the Naval Base Dispensary.

           JOHN C. STEWART
           ENS   USN

20–24   Moored as before. 2005 ENS JOHN C. STEWART, USN returned on board having been TAD to U.S. Naval Justice School, Newport, Rhode Island since 18 March 1963.

           JOHN C. STEWART
           ENS   USN

---

[3]"The Cuban Crisis: A documentary Record," Headline Series No. 157 (January-February 1963): p. 74.

Later, in December, she operated near Bermuda as part of the Recovery Force for the landing of the "Gemini Space Probe". It was the same year that initial proceedings were entered of *Dostal vs. The United States of America*.

The Dragon (XM-47), a medium antitank assault missile.
Source: U.S. Army Missile Command

III.   *Cruising*

NROTC and Academy midshipmen boarded the *Kennedy* in the summer of 1963 for a seven week training cruise from Bermuda to Sydney and on to Nova Scotia. Although it was a training cruise, it was also a beautiful way to take a vacation.

In Bermuda, an island group in the North Atlantic Ocean which is about 570 miles east of Cape Hatteras, the *Kennedy* crew who were granted shore leave were able to view the luxuriant vegetation on the island, as well as try out the British pubs.

Bermuda was discovered by the Spanish navigator, Juan de Bermudez. Bermudez was shipwrecked there early in the 16th century. Later, many sailors would speculate about the theory of the "Bermuda triangle". A settlement was established by a group of English colonists under the direction of the mariner Sir George Somers when their ship, which was headed for Virginia in the U.S., was also shipwrecked there.

The location of the Bermuda Islands is of considerable strategic importance. The islands were once the winter naval station for both the British North Atlantic and West Indian Squadrons. In 1941, during World War II, areas on the islands were leased to the U.S. for naval and air bases for 99 years (until the year 2040).

The island is a popular resort for Americans, thus tourism, ship repairing and servicing the military bases are major sources of employment.

Nova Scotia is a peninsula and province in Southeastern Canada. It was a part of the French province of Acadia. It was largely populated with New Englanders to be replaced by the exiled French. Its capital, Halifax, was founded in 1749. The *Kennedy* forged up the Atlantic Ocean until she was able to view the Bay of Fundy. She anchored in Halifax for training maneuvers and exercises.

After 1960, a new government in Québec sponsored a "Quiet Revolution" to achieve reformation of institutions and greater French/Canadian determination. But extreme separatist organizations appeared, including the terrorist Front de Libération du Québec (F.L.O.).

As in the U.S., the 1960's saw a surge of social criticism that challenged authority. The liberals, under the diplomat Lester Pearson (Q.V.) were responsive to the public mood. The Pearson Administration implemented "cooperative federalism" which gave Québec and other provinces input in national affairs. It created a Royal Commission, which among other things, investigated the U.S. domination of the economy.

So it was, that the tensions between Canada and the U.S. in 1963 were intensifying and the *Kennedy*, which was anchored near Halifax, aggravated those tensions. Some of the men who took shore leave there reported back to the *Kennedy* that there was, indeed, hostility toward the American sailors and that they assumed it would get worse.

As a result of the Front de Libération, Canadian artists and poets, like Anne Hébert, surged forth with their intense display of talent. Hébert's surrealist works, such as *Les Songes en Équilibre* and *Le Tombeau des Rois*, talked about mental anguish, solitude, and death.

That same summer, the *Kennedy* became the second ship in the Atlantic Fleet to qualify in the operation of the Drone Anti-Submarine Helicopter, which was later used in Vietnam.

Aerial view of the Angus L. MacDonald Bridge
under construction, Halifax, Nova Scotia
Courtesy U.S.N.I.

V. *The Gemini Space Probe*

The Russians, by 1964, had 455 cumulative man-hours of Soviet cosmonauts in space. The United States had a total of 54 man-hours in space.

The U.S. Gemini program was designed to explore and develop technology that would be later used to land on the moon. In May 1961, President Kennedy launched the Apollo program which would land a man on the moon and return him safely to Earth before the year 2000. This major NASA commitment resulted in a huge, manned flight program.

The Gemini 7 carried Lt. Col. Frank Borman and Commander James A. Lovell, Jr. It was built to operate for longer periods of time and to develop rendez-vous and landing capabilities and to dock with other spacecraft. Between 1965 and 1966, there were 10 manned Gemini flights.

Air Force Major Edward H. White, II (Gemini 4) was the first U.S. astronaut to walk in space. He spent a little over 20 minutes in space by using a pressurized gas jet maneuvering device.

In December 1965, Geminis 6 and 7 were in orbit together and they rendez-voused within a few feet of each other.

Gemini 6, with Air Force Major Thomas P. Stafford and Captain Schirra on board, landed, and Gemini 7 went on to spend a total of 334 hours in orbit. The two week flight enabled scientific research concerning medical data, which was necessary for the success of the 10-day Apollo mission. It also demonstrated the ability of complex systems such as hydrogen-oxygen fuel-cell electric power and reaction controls.

November, 1966 brought an end to the Gemini Space Probe and along with it, U.S. astronauts had accumulated almost 2,000 man-hours in space, which finally exceeded the Soviet total.

In mid-November 1966, the Gemini 12 probe with Commander Lovell and

Astronauts Frank Borman (right) and James. A. Lovell, Jr.
after the Gemini 7 splash down on December 18, 1965
Photo courtesy of NASA.

Air Force Major Edwin E. Aldrin, Jr., landed near Bermuda. It was the last of the 10 successful probes that began on June 3, 1965.

At sea, waiting to recover the Gemini and her astronauts, was the very excited and proud crew of the *U.S.S. J.P. Kennedy, Jr.*, unfailing yet again in an extraordinary Naval mission.

On July 20, 1969, Apollo 11, carrying astronauts Neil A. Armstrong and Major Aldrin and Collins, landed on the moon. About 47 pounds of rock samples were collected and the American flag was placed there as millions of people on Earth watched on live television.

Commander J.W. Hayes, Jr. of the *U.S.S. J.P. Kennedy, Jr.* could not have been happier. In June, 1969, the Navy settled the lawsuit with the Dostal's and one month later, in July, Hayes said, "the United States has just done the biggest real estate deal of the century" (landing on the moon).

PART II

Newport Naval Base

V. *<u>The Fall</u>*

The bite of the freezing water pulled her to consciousness. She was about 10 to 15 feet below the water's surface. Though in shock, her body automatically responded by fighting its way to the top. Upon her impact with the air, her arms flailed and she screamed hysterically. Soon a sailor was holding her above the water, as he was trying desperately to put a life preserver on her. Then she was hoisted up the side of the *Kennedy* while she continued to gasp for breath.

When she reached the main deck she was taken out of the life preserver and was miraculously alive. Miraculously, because when she went overboard she had fallen between the *U.S.S. J.P. Kennedy, Jr.* and the *U.S.S. Forest Sherman.* Her descent was broken momentarily when her back collided with the *Sherman.* This in itself could have caused a concussion and/or death or drowning. The Officers and Seamen were in a reserved state of shock. This was the *Kennedy*! One of the most noted U.S. destroyers in the world. How could something like this happen?

After much inquiry, it was later learned that the lifeline had not been secured properly, thus, her fall was not protected.

After she had been rescued, she was brought to sick bay and treated by Paladachuck, HMI. She was then taken by ambulance under the custody of Pitts, HMSN, to the Naval Base Hospital.

Not only was she in a traumatized condition, but in excruciating pain. It was later stated in the resulting lawsuit which was captioned:

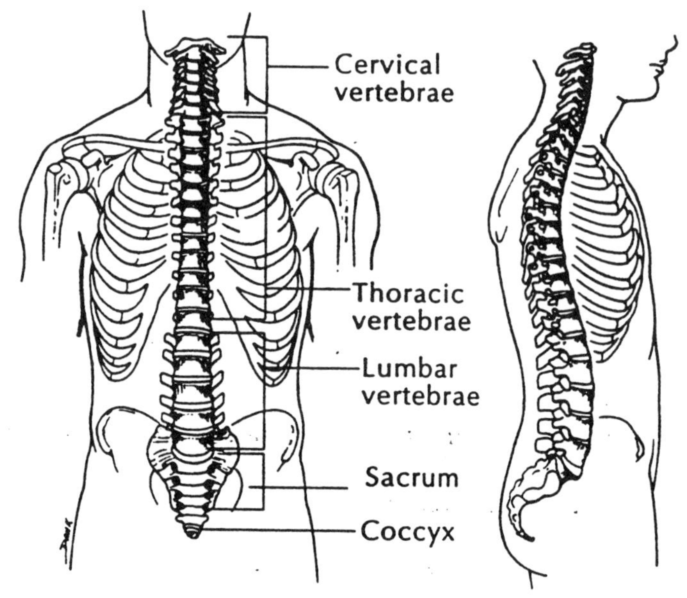

Side and frontal views of the coccyx (tailbone)

Newport Naval Base,
Newport, Rhode Island

CLAIRE DOSTAL,
Plaintiff

v.

THE UNITED STATES OF AMERICA
Defendant

that "the negligence of the defendant, its agents, servants, employees, officers and crew members as herein before alleged was the proximate cause of injuries to plaintiff as follows: fracture of the sacrum, lumbosacral sprain, contusion of the spine, head, thighs, shoulder blades, lower back and left hand; plaintiff was in shock for a period of time after the accident; plaintiff was unconscious at the time she was removed from the water; plaintiff was treated for exposure; plaintiff is at present unmarried but has been advised that as a result of the accident she may experience difficulties during pregnancy and childbirth." The above statement was provided as a part of the complaint as the result of the findings of Doctors Edwin T. Wyman, Irving Glick, Harold L. Temple, Arthur V. Grickey, Peter LeMotte, and Walter A.L. Thompson.

VI.   *The Rescue*

Claire Dostal was a freshman at a college in Boston when she fell off *the J.P. Kennedy Jr.* in Newport, R.I. She and her roommate, "Corky" were the guests of two young seamen, Carmody SMSA and "Red". It was an exciting adventure for the pair to travel to Newport from Boston. They were on a bus whose route went through Providence, R.I., past imaginings of witchhunts and covens, and into the remains of the 16th & 17th centuries. Newport, by comparison, was dotted with historic mansions, churches, yacht basins, and the Newport Naval Base.

On that day, Claire was wearing a white silk blouse with black dots and a black pleated skirt. She wore black shoes and carried a black purse. When she was rescued from the water she was without her purse and shoes which became forever a part of the Narragansett Bay.

It seemed to be an eternity as she was slowly hoisted alongside the destroyer. 10 ft., 20 ft., on and on. The tension bled in the May air. No one knew if she was going to make it. Carmody could barely believe this was all happening. He watched over the side as she came closer and closer to the deck. Men were yelling orders, "Get the sick bay ready, man overboard! Man overboard! Alert the sick bay!"

Somehow she had managed not to swallow any water which was an act of God. Her labored breathing was the result of holding her breath for so long while under the water. By this time, men had amassed on the port side of the ship witnessing the rescue mission. There were whispers and shouts and commanding orders. Finally, she was on board. Two officers held each arm as the life preserver was removed from her and she was slowly escorted with Corky to sick bay for medical attention.

Although the accident was a result of an incidence of negligence, the rescue was an heroic effort to save this young woman's life. The Navy's account of the rescue was less dramatic: "A crew member of the vessel climbed on to a fender alongside the vessel. The crew member, Richard J. Costa, Seaman, caught Miss Claire Dostal's arm and held her while another

Mock Attack on "enemy" submarine is conducted by Navy ship crewmen with realistic new anti-submarine warfare attack trainer at the Fleet Training Center, U.S. Navy Base, Newport, R.I. Source: Lewis, Saunders Byoir & Associates, Inc. 1968.

crew member, Donald E. Vander Woude, lowered a life ring to her. She was then lifted to the vessel's main deck by Costa, Vander Woude, and another crew member whose identify is unknown."

At that moment of rescue, Claire became icily aware of mortality. Years would pass before she could step on a boat or yet alone, sail. Ironically, in the early 1980's, her first time back on a yacht was in Annapolis, on the Chesapeake Bay, near the United States Naval Academy.

VII.   *The Naval Base Hospital*

Corky went to Sick Bay with Claire. There the Navy gave her a robe and Corky helped her to undress so that the staff could dry her clothes. Her skin had turned blue and she was shivering. Paladachuc, Hospitalman 1st Class, ordered an assistant to give her a shot of whiskey to help restore her circulation. She was in so much pain that she couldn't sit down, but rather, had to lie down on the cot that they had provided. After an hour or so, when her clothes were dry, she was taken on a stretcher to an ambulance with Pitts.

In the ambulance, she was not strapped into the stretcher. As the vehicle sped to the hospital, it careened around a corner and she fell off the stretcher, which further injured her. She was assisted back onto the stretcher and then strapped in. She was in so much pain that the fall really didn't seem to make much difference.

The Naval Hospital is located adjacent to the Coasters Harbor Island section of the Naval Base, on the corner of 3rd and Cyprus Streets, Newport, R.I. (near the Newport Bridge ramp). This is a fully-accredited regional hospital providing general clinical services and hospitalization for all military elements in the Narragansett Bay Area, including units of the U.S. Atlantic Fleet. It also renders in- and out-patient care to retired personnel and eligible dependents, and furnishes information and guidance in relation to the Civilian Health and Medical Program for the Uniformed Services.

When they arrived at the hospital, Pitts gave Dr. Green a report which detailed the accident and the initial finding from sick bay by Paladachuc (shock, contusions, pain).

Dr. Martin ordered x-rays of her sacro-iliac to determine the nature of the injuries. She was also externally examined for contusions, intrusive injuries, cuts or other wounds. The medical attention was of several hours' duration and Claire found the ordeal to be exhausting.

After Drs. Arness and Martin reviewed the extent of the injuries, she was medicated with Darven and Basal Mendan.

At long last she was taken back to the Base Motel, where she and Corky had checked into separate rooms when they had arrived in Newport.

The ordeal still wasn't over. She entered her room and just as she collapsed on the bed, there was a knock on the door. It was her friend, Tim Carmody, along with the Naval Station Security Investigator, John Aluza.

Aluza told Corky that he would ask her questions separately so the investigation wouldn't be coerced. He had already taken a statement from Carmody and allowed him to remain in the room.

Claire was exhausted and still in a state of shock. Aluza said, "I'm sorry, but you do not have much choice about answering these questions. This accident occurred on Federal property, so you will have to cooperate."

Later, he went to Corky's room alone to interrogate her. Tim stayed with Claire that night (they were close friends, having grown up together on Long Island). She was so ill that he was reluctant to leave her alone.

The next time Claire saw Corky was in the morning when they were to be escorted to Boston by the Navy.

VIII.   *The Escort*

The phone was ringing in room number 8 at the Base Motel. A sleepy female voice with a Southern drawl answered. "Hello?" "Corky? It's Claire. Did I wake you up?" "Sort of. I had a lousy night. How are you feeling?" "I can barely move. I have no purse, y'know. Can I borrow some make-up? " "Yeah, sure. Give me half an hour and I'll come over to your room." "The Navy's driving us back to Boston. They're picking us up at 9 AM at my room, so bring your suitcase, too. Did you see Red last night?" "No, it's a long story.... I'll tell you back at the dorm." Corky hung up.

Claire distinctively sensed that Corky was conversing in a peculiar, flat monotone, when usually she spoke in her sing-song Southern twang. Oh well, she thought, we've had quite a disastrous weekend. And it was odd, too, that she didn't see Red. She and Red had been dating since Christmas. Most of the time Tim and Red would go to visit the co-eds in Boston on weekend passes. This had been Claire's second trip to Newport and Corky's first.

Going back through Providence wasn't intriguing at all, like the trip down.   But the sailor driving the Naval escort car turned out to be entertaining.

"What are you gals studying in college?"   "I'm studying architecture. My grandfather was an architect and my other grandfather created the art deco on the top of the Chrysler Building in New York. He was actually right out there on top of the building and then he died of pneumonia from the exposure. I think he was about 32. "Anyway, I'm studying architecture, but I don't think I'll pursue it. I like fine art," answered Claire.

"What about the Southern Bell? What are you doing?"

"I'm dating a lot. Boston is great, there's guys everywhere. But I'm not real thrilled about the Boston strangler being out there, too. That's *really* creepy. Studying? I don't know. I'm sort of taking general courses,

I don't know. Where's your family from?" asked Corky.

The sailor said that he was from Ohio somewhere. He was married and had a baby girl. He was going to be discharged in September after his two-year tour of duty. He sounded like he really missed his family and said that the last time he was home was in December for Christmas.

"Do you mind if we smoke?" asked Claire. "Not if you don't mind if I do!" he answered.

"Are you allowed to smoke while you're on duty?" "Sure!" "Well, I think that's all gonna change someday, because people are starting to get picky about smoking" Claire said. "It's ridiculous," Corky agreed.

At that point they were just pulling up to 262 Commonwealth Avenue in Boston where the dorm was.

"Now you girls try to stay out of trouble, O.K.?"

The girls laughed and thanked him for the ride.

PART THREE

In Boston

IX.   <u>*The Rape*</u>

Finally, after arriving back to the safety of the dorm, they both took a deep breath.

"Jesus Christ! What an experience!" summarized Corky.

Claire thought that she was still acting peculiar. She seemed nervous and she smoked a lot. She didn't say much while she unpacked. "You want me to help you unpack, Claire?" "No, I'll be O.K., it's just overnight stuff. I can't wait to change these damn clothes. Y'know, after the accident, all I could think of was when they were pulling me up in the life preserver, do you think they could see up my skirt? It was really embarrassing." Corky laughed, "Christ! At a moment like that—who'd care?" "Yeah, you're right, but I was still embarrassed." "I've got to get relaxed, I'm going over to the Greek's for a beer, wanna come?" "No, my back really hurts now after sitting in that escort car for two hours. I'm just going to lie down for awhile and I guess I ought to call my mother." "O.K., see ya later." "Oh! Corky, would you bring me back a pack of Marlboros?" "Yeah, sure."

"Hello, Operator?" "Yes." "I'd like to make a person-to-person, collect call to Clara Dostal, from Claire. Her number is: area code 516, Hunter 2-2612M." "Please hold. Hello, will you accept a collect call from Claire?" "Yes." "Go ahead."

"Hello?" "Mom?, I have a problem. There was this accident." "What??" "Well,, I went down to Newport with Corky to see Timmie and Red..." "How did you get a weekend pass?" "Well, the same way I got off for the Jewish holidays in high school... I forged your signature." "What was the accident?" "Well, you won't believe this, but I fell off a destroyer."

18

"Oh? My God!" "Are you O.K.? Are you in the hospital, what..?" "I'm back at the dorm. The Navy brought us back. My back is all black and blue and I'm really in a lot of pain, and the Darven they gave me isn't working." "Well, I'm going to call Dr. Glick tomorrow. I can't reach him on a Sunday. You better rest. Maybe you better not go to classes tomorrow." "I wasn't planning to go."

A couple of hours later, Corky came back with the cigarettes. She had had a few beers at the Greek's and was a little bit cheerier. She flopped on to her bed.

"What a mess! What a goddamn mess!"

"What are you talking about, Corky?"

"I never got to see Red, I stood him up. I was supposed to meet him for dinner Saturday night." "Why didn't you? Timmie and me thought you were out with him." Claire lit a cigarette and thought for a moment. Corky didn't answer her. Suddenly Corky started crying. Not hysterically, just sort of whimpering like a puppy. Sniffling. "Corky?" "I don't want to talk about it." "Corky! What happened? Isn't it bad enough that I fell off the ship?" "Jesus, Claire, I don't know what to do." "To *do*? To do about what? Red? Why didn't you meet Red?" Then she yelled, "Because he raped me! That goddam son-of-a-bitch asking the questions, the questions about you falling overboard... he invited me out to dinner to ask me the questions, and then he took me back to the Base Motel, and he raped me!"

"Oh, my God! Oh, God, Corky, No."

X.	*Underline: United States v. Short*

In the United States Court of Military Appeals, 1954, a general court-martial in Japan convicted the accused of assault with intent to commit rape, and sentenced him to a dishonorable discharge, total forfeitures, and confinement to hard labor for 10 years. The convening authority modified the sentence by reducing the period of confinement to 5 years. A board of review affirmed the conviction and the modified sentence.

The events in the case took place on November 28, 1952 in Tokyo. At about 11:30 p.m., two Japanese girls, Yayoi Tomobe and Tokiko Okano, left the shop in which they worked to dispose of some waste paper in a public latrine located across the street. Apparently as the girls were crossing the street, they were approached from behind by the accused (Short) and his companion, Private O'Rourke. From their speech, Okano deducted that the "foreigners" were intoxicated. She was frightened. Calling out to Tokiko to run, Okano ran back to the shop. Tomobe, however, tripped over a stone. As she regained her balance, she was caught under her right arm by the accused. The accused spoke to her in English. Although she had learned some English in school., she was "so scared and...surprised" that she did not know what was said, except that there was mention of yen. She was then pulled to the front of the latrine and pushed in. The accused entered and closed the door.

Tomobe tried to get away from the accused, but he was "very big". She was "scared" and "had no strength to go out." While the accused did not punch, kick, or otherwise inflict bodily harm upon her, he fondled her person against her protests. She kept saying, "No" in Japanese as loudly as she could. She pushed the accused away, but he was "so strong that [she] was unable to hold him away."

In the meantime, Okano, having seen Tomobe pulled into the Latrine, reported to the manger of the shop. He immediately went to the latrine and opened the door. He heard Tomoke saying, "No," and he saw the accused holding her. However, just then O'Rourke tapped him on the shoulder and he made no further effort to interfere. Instead, he went to a police box, located approximately four feet from the latrine, and reported the matter to the Japanese police. They hastened to the latrine. One of the policemen opened the door, and in Japanese called out to the accused to stop. In the same language, the accused replied that it was all right. Then he was forcibly removed from the latrine and taken to a police box.

At the trial, the accused admitted fondling Tomobe, as set out in the specification. However, he denied that he acted unlawfully. He testified that when he saw Tomobe, he thought that she was a prostitute since the area was known to be frequented by them. He "propositioned" her, and after some negotiation they agreed on a price of 500 yen. Tomobe showed him the latrine; he previously did not know of its existence. Inside, Tomobe helped him in his efforts to "make love to her". Although he was "under the influence," he was generally aware of what he was doing. When the police entered the latrine he thought that they wanted to arrest the girl as a prostitute. He told them that it was all right because he was anxious to protect her.

Before giving his instructions, the law officer discussed them with both counsel in a recorded out-of-court hearing. Each counsel submitted requests for specific instructions. With some modification, one of the three offered by the prosecution was accepted; the two submitted by the defense were rejected. The defense requests were as follows:

"The essential elements of non-consent, or that the act be against the woman's will, signifies that it be committed against the utmost reluctance and resistance which the women is capable of making at the time".

"In order to constitute an offense, the accused must think the victim is not consenting because he must intend not only to have carnal knowledge of the woman but to do so by force."

"The guilt or innocence of the accused depends on the circumstances as they appear to him..."[4]

---

[4]*Criminal Law and its Processes*, by Sanford H. Kadish and Conrad G. Paulsen, pp. 223-225.

XI.   *The Investigator*

"Corky, you've got to report this to the police!" "I can't." "Why not?"

They were having dinner at a seafood restaurant near the naval base. The investigator asked Corky what she would like to drink. "Why, I'm Southern, you know, so I'll have a bourbon and water." "Well, I'll be... that's my favorite..."

After several rounds of drinks, the two ordered dinner. It wasn't until a little after eleven o'clock, when they left the restaurant. He drove her back to the Base Motel. "Would ya like a night cap?" Corky inquired. "Sure!" He came into the room. She poured two glasses of bourbon.

"So you didn't really see Dostal go overboard did you?" "Yes, I did!" He moved closer to her. "I don't think you understand what I'm saying. You did not see her fall off the ship." "But I did!" He grabbed her by the arm. "Let me go!"

"Let me tell you something, lady, I'm a Federal officer, and you'll do what I tell you to. And if you say anything against me, I'll tell them that you're a goddam prostitute."

He reached into his pants pocket and pulled out a twenty dollar bill and threw it in her face. Corky was speechless. She felt trapped and helpless. He was blackmailing her and she couldn't do anything about it. She was afraid to scream or to fight him off. He was armed with a gun. She decided to just play along with it until she could get him to leave.

"Take your clothes off bitch..." Eventually it was over. Before he left her room he said, "Just remember, Kiddo, if you say anything to anybody about this, I'll get you into the slammer for hooking." He turned around and shut the door. It was about 2 a.m.

"Don't you see, Claire, he has me trapped. I can't talk about this, and you can't either...ever. Promise me you won't!"

> "Now these are the laws of the Navy
> And many and varied are they
> But the hull and the deck and the keel
> And the truck of the law is—OBEY."[5]

In 1963 there were no rape crisis centers where Corky could go. For a few days she just hung around the dorm and sulked. She never called her parents until later and that was only to tell them she was quitting school and coming home.

On Monday, May 10th, Claire's mother called her. Claire was still not able to attend classes because of the back injury. The main reason was that her classes were spread in buildings in an area of about 10 blocks. She tried to walk to one of her classes, but wound up in excruciating pain. She did not know it at the time, but she actually had a fractured coccyx (tailbone). This had not been detected at the Naval hospital when they took x-rays. Drs. Martin, Green and Arness determined that the x-rays were inconclusive. Dr. Glick, a New York civilian orthopedic physician later took x-rays of the area and determined *conclusively* that her coccyx *was* fractured.   The tailbone was bent inward, pressing on her womb. Consequently, Dr. Glick's diagnosis concluded that "due to this repositioning, it appears that the patient will have great difficulty with childbirth if she chooses to bear children..."

---

[5]From: The Laws of the Navy
     by Admiral R.A. Hopwoood

XII.   *Going Home*

After explaining to her mother about the difficulty of getting to classes, her mother called the College Dean and explained the situation. The Dean, upon reviewing Claire's records for the year, assured her mother that she would get credit for the full year and that she was free to go home two weeks prior to the semester end.

Claire told Corky the good news. "Well, I'm not going to stay here, either!" Corky called her parents and told them about Claire's accident and told them she was coming home. Evidently, they were pretty lenient and said it was o.k.

On their last day in Boston, Wednesday, May 12, they decided to do the town like tourists. They were leaving to go home on Thursday morning.

They had been in Boston for nearly nine months and had never really seen the city. They had been to loads of frat parties and to Filene's department store, to restaurants and college hang-outs, but had not been aware of the museums, monuments and libraries there.

First they went to the Boston Museum of Fine Arts, which held Oriental, French and early American works. Then on to the Isabella Stewart Gardner Museum, the Museum of Science and the Hayden Planetarium. They didn't get to see the John F. Kennedy Memorial Library, for it was completed in 1979 at the Boston Campus of the University of Massachusetts. It contains the archives and memorabilia of President John F. Kennedy (q.v.).

They were given a tour of one museum that provided a brief history of Massachusetts. In 1602 the English navigator Bartholomew Gasnold (q.v.) established a small settlement on Cuttyhunk Island, between Buzzard's Bay and Vineyard Sound, but the little settlement was abandoned after three weeks. Later, a group of about 100 pilgrims who were from Leiden in the Netherlands made a successful attempt at colonization. They were Puritans, also known as Separatists, who had fled from England to the Netherlands to escape persecution in 1608. It was the intention of the Puritans to settle south of the Hudson River, but bad weather drove their ship to the neighborhood of Cape Cod. There the group drew up the Mayflower Compact and elected John Carver (q.v.) governor for one year.

On December 21, 1620, the emigrants landed at Plymouth. After several years of privation, the settlement was founded. In 1624, the property of the colonies, which was held in common, was divided among the settlers. In 1629, a patent confirming the Colonists' right to the territory was issued to Governor William Bradford (q.v.).

By the early 1900's, home manufacture was securely established in the textile, whaling, leather and metal industries. But Massachusetts, especially Boston, was hit hard by the depression in the 1930's. The economy revived during World War II, when factories there produced vast quantities of war materials, including destroyers. With the post-war decline, the State became a leading center for rocket research and the production of electronics equipment. In fact, the tuning fork, timing device for the Gemini Space Probe had been built in Boston, although it had been designed in New York.

"Well, that museum history tour about Massachusetts was really interesting. But I'm really not sorry that I won't be coming back," Claire remarked.

View of the downtown skyline of Boston,
largest city and Capital of Massachusetts

XIII.   *The Complaint*

TO THE HONORABLE JUDGES OF
THE UNITED STATES DISTRICT
COURT FOR THE SOUTHERN DISTRICT OF NEW YORK

The Libel and Complaint of
CLAIRE DOSTAL, by
CLARA DOSTAL and
FRANK DOSTAL

-against-

THE UNITED STATES of America,
as Owner and Operator of the
U.S.S. JOSEPH P. KENNEDY, JR.
(DD-850), in a cause of tort
or damage, civil and maritime
alleges upon information and
belief and respectfully shows
to this Honorable Court as
follows:

<u>AS AND FOR A FIRST CAUSE OF ACTION ON BEHALF OF</u>

<u>LIBELANT, CLAIRE DOSTAL</u>:

FIRST: Libelant Claire Dostal is an infant over the age of

18 years, and is a citizen of the United States of America and a resident of

the State of New York.

SECOND: Clara Dostal is the mother of said Claire Dostal

and has legal custody of said Claire Dostal, and is a citizen of the United

27

States of America and a resident of the State of New York.

THIRD: This action is brought on behalf of Claire Dostal by Clara Dostal, her mother.

FOURTH: Libelant Frank Dostal is the father of said Claire Dostal, and is a citizen of the United States of America and a resident of the State of New York.

FIFTH: Respondent The United States of America is a corporate sovereign, which at all times hereinafter mentioned was the owner of a vessel known as the U.S.S. Joseph P. Kennedy, Jr. (DD-850), and which has consented to be sued herein pursuant to the provisions of the Public Vessels Act, 46 U.S.C. Sections 781-790.

SIXTH: At all times hereinafter mentioned, respondent operated and was in control and in possession of the U.S.S. Joseph P. Kennedy, Jr. (DD-850).

SEVENTH: On or about May 3, 1963, libelant Claire Dostal was a guest aboard the U.S.S. Joseph P. Kennedy, Jr., having come aboard at the invitation and request of a member of the crew of said vessel.

EIGHTH: Respondents' vessel, the U.S.S. Joseph P.

Kennedy, Jr. was, at the time of the occurrence hereinafter alleged, moored in the navigable waters of Narragansett Bay at the U.S. Naval Station, Newport, Rhode Island.

NINTH: While libelant, Claire Dostal, was lawfully and properly aboard respondent's vessel as the invited guest of a member of the crew of said vessel, she was caused to fall overboard, striking her back against an adjoining vessel and thereafter being immersed in water, when a lifeline or guard rail gave way, thereby sustaining the injuries and loss of personal properties hereinafter alleged.

TENTH: The aforesaid occurrence and the injuries and loss of personal properties resulting therefrom were caused wholly and solely by the carelessness, recklessness and negligence of respondent, its agents, servants and employees, in the following respects, among others, to be proved upon the trial hereof: failing and neglecting to provide libelant with a safe place in which to visit and walk about the vessel; failing to properly secure and maintain the deck and appurtenances of said vessel, including the guard rails, life lines and stanchions; failing to maintain said vessel and the portions thereof open to visitors in a reasonably proper and safe condition; and failing to properly supervise the area and failing to properly inspect the conditions in and about the area where libelant was caused to fall overboard. Libelants reserve the right to allege further faults if after so advised.

ELEVENTH: It is the duty of respondent to provide libelant with a safe and seaworthy vessel, and to further provide libelant with a safe area to visit.

TWELFTH: By reason of the premises, libelant Claire Dostal was rendered sick, sore, lame and disabled, and she suffered emotional shock and injury to her head, back and spine from which she is still suffering and which is believed to be permanent and she suffered, and she still suffers from severe pain and other conditions resulting from the aforesaid occurrence, and said libelant required and will continue to require medical care, all to her in a sum presently estimated to be $75,000, no part of which has been paid although the same has been duly demanded. Libelants reserve the right to increase this amount if later so advised.

THIRTEENTH: All and singular the premises are true, and within the admiralty and maritime jurisdiction of the United States of America and of this Honorable Court.

<u>AS AND FOR A SECOND CAUSE OF ACTION, ON BEHALF OF LIBELANT, CLAIRE DOSTAL</u>:

FOURTEENTH: Libelant repeats and realleges with the same force and effect as if herein set forth at length each and every allegation contained in articles First through Twelfth of the Libel.

FIFTEENTH: By reason of the premises, libelant lost personal properties all to her damage in the sum of $300, no part of which has been paid, although the same has been duly demanded.

SIXTEENTH: All and singular the premises are true, and within the admiralty and maritime jurisdiction of the United States of America and of this Honorable Court.

<u>AS AND FOR A THIRD CAUSE OF ACTION, ON BEHALF OF LIBELANT, FRANK DOSTAL</u>:

SEVENTEENTH: Libelant repeats and realleges with the same force and effect as if herein set forth at length each and every allegation contained in articles First through Twelfth of this Libel.

EIGHTEENTH: By reason of the premises, libelant, Frank Dostal, has necessarily expended large sums of money for medical care and treatment of his said infant daughter, and has further expended monies for his daughter's subsistence and education which was interrupted by reason of the facts alleged in the premises, and will hereafter necessarily expend large sums of money for further medical care and treatment, all to libelant's damage in amount presently estimated to be $10,000. No part of which has been paid although the same has been duly demanded. Libelant reserves the right to amend this amount if later so advised.

NINETEENTH: All and singular the premises are true, and within the admiralty and maritime jurisdiction of the United States of America and of this Honorable Court.

<u>AS AND FOR A FOURTH CAUSE OF ACTION, ON BEHALF OF LIBELANT, CLARA DOSTAL</u>:

TWENTIETH: Libelant repeats and realleges with the same force and effect as is herein set forth at length each and every allegation contained in articles First through Twelfth of this Libel.

TWENTY FIRST: By reason of the premises, libelant, Clara Dostal, has necessarily expended large sums of money for medical care for her infant daughter, and has further expended monies for her infant daughter's subsistence and education which was interrupted by reason of the facts alleged in the premises and will hereafter necessarily spend large sums of money for further medical care and treatment, and she has been deprived of the services of her daughter and libelant, Clara Dostal, has been informed and believes that such impairment and deprivation will continue for a long time to come, all of libelant's damage in an amount presently estimated to be $10,000, no part of which has been paid although the same has been duly demanded. Libelant reserves the right to amend this amount if later so advised.

TWENTY SECOND: All and singular the premises are true, and within the admiralty and maritime jurisdiction of the United States of America and of this Honorable Court.

WHEREFORE, libelant Claire Dostal, by libelant Clara Dostal, demands judgment against respondent in the sum of $75,300; libelant Frank Dostal demands judgment against respondent in the sum of $10,000; and libelant Clara Dostal demands judgment against the respondent in the sum of $10,000; all with interest, and the costs and disbursements of this action;

and libelants further pray that they may have such other, further or different

relief as may be just in the premises.

HAIGHT, GARDNER, POOR & HAVENS
Proctors for Libelants
80 Broad Street
New York, N.Y. 10004.

STATE OF NEW YORK)
: ss.:
COUNTY OF NEW YORK)

      CHARLES S. HAIGHT, JR., being duly sworn, deposes and says:

      1.   I am associated with the firm of Haight, Gardner, Poor & Havens, proctors for the libelants herein. I have read the foregoing Libel, and the same is true to the best of my information and belief. The source of my information and the grounds for my belief are documents and statements furnished by the libelants.

      2.   The reason I make this verification, and not the libelants, is that none of the libelants are presently within the jurisdiction of this Honorable Court.

____

/S/

[CHARLES S. HAIGHT, JR.]

Sworn to before me this
30th day of April, 1965.

   /S/

____
Notary Public
Margaret E. Dillemuth
Notary Public, State of New York

PART FOUR

Dostal v. United States of America

XIV.	*Interrogatories*

Plaintiff: 1.   At the time of the occurrence alleged in the complaint herein, were visitors permitted to come on board the U.S.S. Joseph P. Kennedy, Jr.?

Defendant: Yes.

Plaintiff: 2.   If the answer to the foregoing interrogatory is in the affirmative, state:

    (a) What persons were permitted to visit the U.S.S. J.P. Kennedy, Jr..

    (b) The hours of the day during May 3, 1963, when such visitors were permitted on board the vessel.

    (c) The areas of the vessel where visitors were permitted to go;

    (d) The substance of any directions or instructions given to such visitors in connection with their visit;

    (e) The manner in which such directions or instructions were communicated to such visitors.

Defendant: (a) Persons having business with the ship or its personnel and friends and relatives of crew members.

    (b) No definite hours were set.

    (c) Visitors were to be escorted and not allowed in restricted areas.

    (d) No specific directions or instructions were given.

    (e) See the Answer to interrogatory 2(d) above.

Plaintiff: 3:   Did any visitors go on Board the U.S.S. Joseph P. Kennedy, Jr. on May 3, 1963? If so, state:

	(a) How many;
	(b) Whether plaintiff Claire Dostal visited the vessel that day.
Defendant:	Visitors did call on board the U.S.S. Joseph P. Kennedy, Jr. on May 3.
	(a) Number of visitors is unknown.
	(b) Plaintiff, Claire Dostal, did visit the U.S.S. Joseph P. Kennedy, Jr. on May 3, 1963.
Plaintiff 4:	State the name, rank, present duty station, or last known address of any person known to defendant who:
	(a) Witnessed an accident involving plaintiff Claire Dostal on board the U.S.S. Joseph P. Kennedy, Jr. on May 3, 1963.
	(b) Witnessed or participated in efforts to rescue plaintiff Claire Dostal from the waters of Narragansett Bay;
	(c) Witnesses who participated in medical attention given to plaintiff Claire Dostal thereafter.
Defendant:	(a) Timothy M. Carmody, Signalman Seaman Douglas E. Vander Woude, Interior Communicationsman First Class Richard J. Costa, Ensign Roger Loren Allen, Boatswain's Mate Seaman Marvin F. Bringhurst, Signalman Second Class (b) Donald E. Vander Woude, Interior Communicationsman Richard Costa, Ensign Roger Loren Allen, Boatswain's Mate Seaman Marvin F. Bringhurst, Signalman Second Class James B. Rucker, Lieutenant Timothy Carmody, Signalman Seaman William F. Paladechuck, Hospitalman First Class Mary Ann Jones, Civilian

(c) William F. Paladechuck, Hospitalman First Class
Mary Ann Jones, Civilian
Dr. William Martin, Lieutenant Commander, Medical Corps
Dr. S.L. Green, Lieutenant, Medical Corps
Dr. John A. Arness, Lieutenant, Medical Corps
Frederick G. Pitts, Hospitalman

Plaintiff: 5:   Did the United States Navy, or any other agency or entity under the control of defendant, conduct an inquiry or investigation into the accident referred to in the complaint herein? If so, state:

(a) The date such inquiry or investigation was commenced;

(b) The date when it was completed;

(c) The name, rank, present duty station, or last known address of the officers or persons constituting the board of investigation or inquiry;

(d) Whether the proceedings were transcribed and if so, the present location of the transcript;

(e) The name, rank, present duty station, or last known address of each witness who appeared before such inquiry or investigation;

(f) The name, rank, present duty station, or last known address of any person who submitted a written statement in connection with such inquiry or investigation;

(g) The nature and present location of copies of the written statements prepared by the persons referred to in the Answer to sub-interrogation (f) above.

Defendant: Yes.

(a) An investigation made by the U.S. Naval Station, Newport, R.I. Security Office personnel was initiated on May 3, 1963. Another investigation made pursuant to order of the vessel's Commanding Officer, commenced on May 6, 1963.

(b) The investigation made by Security Office personnel was concluded on the day of the accident. The investigation made by the vessel was completed on May 29,1963.

(c) The Station Security Office investigation was made by John F. Aluza, Naval Station Security Office Investigator. Commander William J. Longhi, USN was the investigating officer of the investigation conducted by the vessel.

(d) The proceedings were not transcribed. A report of investigation was made by the investigating officer, Lieutenant Commander William J. Longi and a copy of that report is held by the Admiralty and Shipping Section, department of Justice, New York, N.Y.

(e) The following named persons appeared before the Naval Station:
Security Investigator, John F. Aluza:
Timothy M. Carmody, Signalman Seaman
Mary Ann Jones, Civilian
Plaintiff, Claire Dostal

The following named persons appeared before the investigating officer, Lieutenant Commander William J. Longhi:
Roger Loren Allen, Boatswain's Mate Seaman
Richard J. Costa, Ensign
Marvin F. Bringhurst, Signalman Second Class
Donald E. Vander Woude, Interior
Communicationsman, First Class
James B. Rucker, Jr., Lieutenant
Timothy M. Carmody, Signalman Seaman
William M. Paladechuc, Hospitalman First Class
John L. Roderick, Boatswain's Mate Seaman

(f) See answer to interrogatory 5(d) which is repeated answer.

(g) is held by the Admiralty and Shipping Section, Department of Justice, New York, N.Y.

Plaintiff: 6. With respect to any statements, reports, log books, questionnaires, forms; x-rays, medical records, or other documents relating to or pertaining in any manner to the accident referred to in the complaint, and not previously identified in the answer to these interrogatories, state as to each such document:

(a) The nature thereof;

(b) The name, rank, present duty station of the person preparing the document;

(c) The present location of a true copy thereof.

Defendant: (a) (1) Statement of John L. Rodericks, Boatswain's Mate Seaman and sketch of how quarterdeck area looked just before accident occurred.

(2) U.S. Naval Station, Newport, R.I. Security log with entry as to escorting of station ambulance which took plaintiff from vessel to Naval Dispensary.

(3) Quartermaster's Notebook of USS JOSEPH P. KENNEDY with entry regarding accident.

(4) Daily Medical Journal of USS JOSEPH P. KENNEDY with entry regarding accident and medical attention given to Miss Dostal.

(5) Deck log of the USS JOSEPH P. KENNEDY containing entry regarding accident.

(6) Consultation report of the medical officer of the U.S. Naval Hospital, Newport, R.I., as to medical examination and treatment of Miss Dostal.

(7) Injury report made by medical officer at the U.S. Naval Hospital, Newport, R.I., as to medical exam and treatment of Miss Dostal.

(8) Injury report made by Miss Dostal by medical

officer at the U.S. Naval Base Dispensary, Newport, R.,I. as to medical treatment.

(9) Radiographic report on x-rays taken of plaintiff at the U.S. Naval Hospital, Newport, R.I., on May 3, 1963.

(10) Photograph of area where accident occurred taken after May 3, 1963.

(11) Photograph of hook around which lifeline was wrapped, taken after May 3, 1963.

(12) Sketch of how accident area looked after the accident.

(13) X-rays of plaintiff taken at the U.S. Naval Hospital, Newport, R.I. after the accident.

(b) (1) John L. Rodericks, Boatswain's Mate Seaman.

(2) C. Pierone, Boilertender Chief.

(3) Identity presently unknown.

(4) William M Paladechuck, Hospitalman 1st Class.

(5) D.P. Yonkers Ensign.

(6) Dr. William Marti, Lieutenant Commander.

(7) Dr. John A. Arness, Lieutenant.

(8) Dr. S.L. Green, Lieutenant, Medical Corps.

(9) Identity Unknown.

(10) Identity Unknown.

(11) Identity Unknown.

(12) Roger Loren Allen, Boatswain's Mate Seaman.

(c) True copies of documents referred to in answers (21) through (11) to interrogatories 6(a) and (b) are held by the Admiralty and Shipping Section, Department of Justice, New York, N.Y. Documents referred to in Answers (13) to interrogatories 69(a) and (b) are held by the U.S. Naval Hospital, Newport, R.I., and will be made available.

Plaintiff: 7.   Were the deck and topside areas of the U.S.S. Joseph P.

Kennedy which were accessible to visitors on May 3, 1963, surrounded or enclosed by lifelines or guard rails?

Defendant: Yes.

Plaintiff: 8.   If the answer to the preceding interrogatory is in the affirmative, describe in detail the manner in which such lifelines or guard rails were rigged, with particular reference to:
(a)   The distance between the stanchions or other vertical supporting members;
(b)   The number of lifelines or guard rails;
(c)   The manner in which the life lines or guard rails were secured to the stanchions or other vertical supporting members;
(d)   The height from the deck of each life line or guard rail.
Defendant may confine its answer to the foregoing interrogatory to that section of the U .S.S. Joseph P. Kennedy, Jr. involved in the accident alleged in the complaint.

Defendant: (a)   Presently unknown.
(b)   A single life line with a guard net below.
(c)   The life line which had been broken to allow positioning of a brow on the deck was doubled back and strapped off with a series of half hitches and a square knot. The loop which was made was passed through a hook on the stanchion adjacent to the brow.

(d)   Presently unknown.

Plaintiff: 9.   Did any of the equipment referred to in the answer to the foregoing interrogatory fail at the time of the accident alleged in the Complaint?

Defendant: No.

Plaintiff: 10.   If the answer to the preceding interrogatory is in the affirmative, state: (a) what failed; (b) why it did so.

Defendant: See answer to interrogatory 9.

Plaintiff: 11.   Describe in detail any actions taken by defendant, its agents or employees, to rescue plaintiff Claire Dostal from the waters of Narragansett Bay following the accident alleged in the Complaint.

Defendant: A crew member of the vessel climbed on to a fender alongside the vessel. The crew member, Richard J. Costa, Seaman, caught Miss Claire Dostal's arm and held her while another crew member, Donald E. Vander Woude, lowered a life ring to her. She was then lifted to the vessel's main deck by Costa, Vander Woude and another crew member whose identity is unknown.

Plaintiff: 12.   Following the accident alleged in the complaint, were any repairs or alterations performed to the facilities referred to in the answer to Interrogatory No. 7?

Defendant: Yes.

Plaintiff: 13.   If the answer to the preceding interrogatory is in the affirmative, state:
(a) When such repairs or alterations were made;
(b) What they consisted of;
(c) The reason they were made.

Defendant: (a) After the accident on May 3, 1963.
(b) The life line was passed around the stanchion in addition to being passed through a hook on the stanchion.

(c) To keep the life line from coming off the stanchion.

Plaintiff: 14. Following the accident alleged in the complaint, did defendant or its agents, servants or employees give any medical attention to plaintiff Claire Dostal?

Defendant: Yes.

Plaintiff: 15. If the answer to the preceding interrogatory is in the affirmative, state:
(a) The period of time during which such medical attention was given;
(b) What the medical attention consisted of;
(c) The name, rank, present duty station, of each person concerned in such medical attention;
(d) The observations of conclusions of such persons concerning the physical and mental condition of plaintiff Claire Dostal.

Defendant: (a) Medical attention was given after the accident on May 3, 1963, and was only of a few hours duration. None was given after that date.
(b) Attention given aboard the vessel consisted of warmth, rest and the opportunity for plaintiff to dry her clothes. Plaintiff was then taken by ambulance to the U.S. Navy Dispensary, Newport, R.I. Medical attention at the Dispensary consisted of examination and referral to the U.S. Naval Hospital, Newport, R.I., for consultation. Medical attention given at the U.S. Naval Hospital consisted of examination, x-rays of the sacro-iliac and giving drugs Darven and Basal Mendon.
(c) William M. Paladechuck.
Dr. John A. Arness, Lieutenant, Medical Corps
Dr. W. Martin, Lieutenant Commander, Medical Corps

Dr. S.L. Green, Lieutenant, Medical Corps

(d) No conclusions were made by Paladechuck. Dr. Arness described the nature and extent of injury to plaintiff as contusion of both hips and posterior thighs, hematoma of hips and thighs and exposure. Dr. Martin's diagnosis was contusions of buttock and thighs. Dr. Green reported that examination of the sacrum and coccyx does not demonstrate any definite evidence of a fracture in this region and that examination of the pelvis does not reveal any evidence of any fracture or any bony abnormality.

Plaintiff: 16. Did defendant or its agents or employees take any statements, oral or written, from Plaintiff Claire Dostal following the accident alleged in the Complaint.

Defendant: Yes.

Plaintiff: 17. If the answer to the foregoing interrogatory is in the affirmative, state with respect to each such statement:
(a) The name, rank of the person taking the statement;
(b) Where the statement was taken;
(c) When the statement was taken;
(d) For what purpose the statement was taken;
(e) What use was thereafter made of the statement;
(f) If oral, the substance thereof;
(g) If in writing, the present location of a true copy.

Defendant: (a) John F. Aluza, Base Security Investigator.
(b) U.S. Naval Hospital, Newport, R.I.
(c) May 3, 1963.
(d) Investigation of accident.
(e) The statement was submitted to the investigating officer, Lieutenant Commander William J. Longhi who included it with his report of investigation.
(f) See the answer to interrogatory 17(g).

(g) Plaintiff's statement was taken in writing and a copy is held at the Admiralty and Shipping Section, Department of Justice, New York, N.Y.

Plaintiff: 18.   State the name, rank of:
(a) The officer in command of the U.S.S. Joseph P. Kennedy, Jr. on May 3, 1963;
(b) The senior and junior officers of the deck at the time of the accident alleged in the complaint.

Defendant:
(a) Nicholas Mikhalevsky, Captain.
(b) James B. Rucker, Jr., Lieutenant.
(c) Donald E. Vander Woude, Junior Officer of the Deck;
(d) Marvin Bringhurst, Petty Officer of the Watch.

Plaintiff: 19.   Did defendant or its agents or employees reach any conclusion as to the cause or causes of the accident alleged in the Complaint?

Defendant: No answer required.

Plaintiff: 20.   With respect to the allegation in Paragraph 23 of the answer herein that Claire Dostal's injuries or damages "were caused in whole or in part by plaintiff's own negligence and fault" set forth in detail each and every act on the part of plaintiff which defendant contends was negligent or constituted fault.

Defendant: Plaintiff was among other respects negligent in leaning against the life line.

Plaintiff: 21.   With respect to the use of or reliance upon life lines, guard rails, or comparable equipment, on board the U.S.S. Joseph P. Kennedy, Jr. on May 3, 1963, were any signs posted or instructions given to visitors?

Defendant: None.

Plaintiff: 22.   If the answer to the preceding interrogatory is in the affirmative, describe each such sign or instruction with particularity.

Defendant: No answer required.

Interrogatories submitted June 26, 1967
By the law firm of HAIGHT, GARDNER, POOR &
HAVENS

Answers to Interrogatories submitted
December 8, 1967
By ROBERT MORGENTHAU
United States Attorney
Department of Justice

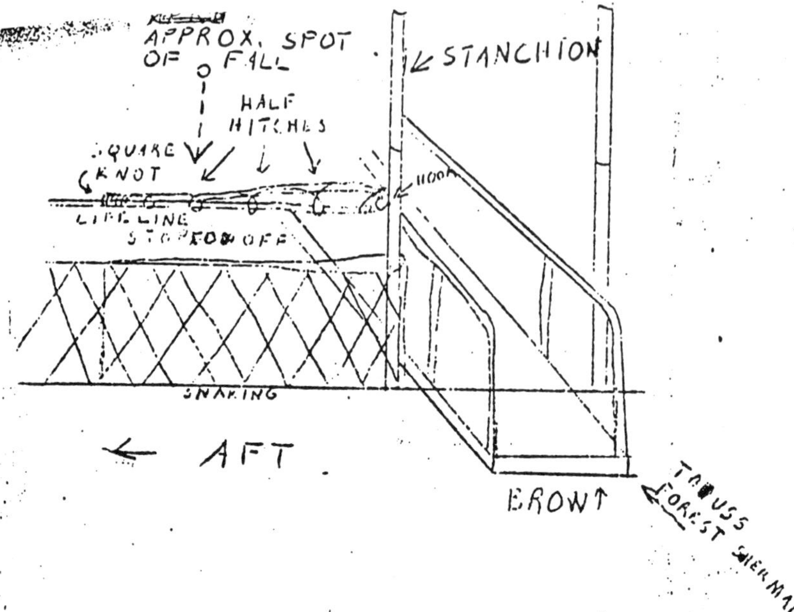

1. My name is John L. RODERICKS, BMSN. I was in charge of rigging the quarterdeck on the evening of 3 May 1963 after the USS JOSEPH P. KENNEDY, JR. (DD 850) returned from sea.

2. This sketch is a reproduction of the portion of the quarterdeck area from which Miss Claire Dostal fell, as it looked on 3 May 1963. The USS FORREST SHERMAN was moored alongside to port.

3. The life line was doubled back and stopped off securely with a series of half hitches and a square knot as shown above. It is unreasonable to conclude that the lifeline could have become untied.

4. The lifeline was passed through the hook on the stanchion as shown above. It is possible that by pushing upward on the lifeline, while leaning into it at the same time, the line could have worked itself out of t, the hook on the stanchion.

5. The above fact are true to the best of my knowledge.

John L. RODERICKS, BMSN, USN

Encl (11)

EXHIBIT "B"

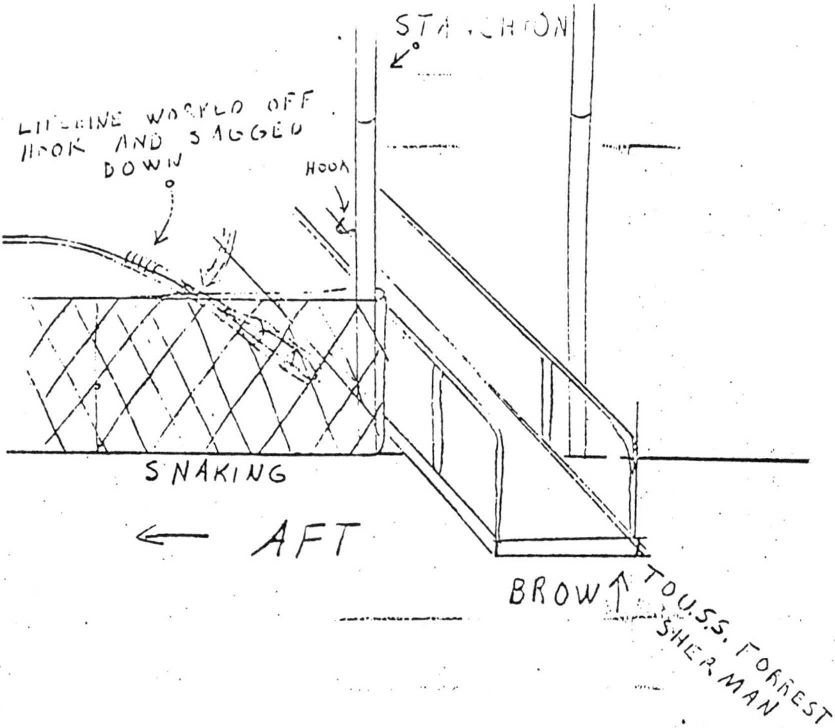

This sketch shows approximately how the qs interdeck of the Kennedy looked after Miss Tootal fell on 3 May 1963

_______ L. Allen
BMSN, USN

28

Encl (21)

EXHIBIT "C"

XV.   *Discovery of Documents*

Introduction

This is an action for personal injuries and property loss, brought against the United States of America under the Public Vessels Act, 46 U.S.C. Sections 781-790.

The action arises out of an accident involving plaintiff Claire Dostal, a minor, while she was a visitor on board a naval destroyer, the U.S.S. Joseph P. Kennedy, Jr., on May 3, 1963.

Plaintiffs now move, pursuant to Rule 34, Federal Rules of Civil Procedure, for discovery of certain pertinent documents in the possession, custody or control of defendant.

The full particulars of the case are set forth in the affidavit of Charles S. Haight, Jr., verified June 27, 1967, submitted in support of the motion.

The documents as to which discovery is sought are specified in the notice of motion.

ARGUMENT

I.

THE RULES PERMIT BROAD
DISCOVERY OF DOCUMENTS.

Rule 34 permits a broad discovery of documents. It provides, in pertinent part:

> "Upon motion of any party showing
> good cause therefore and upon notice to
> all other parties, and subject to the

provisions of Rule 30(b), the court in which an action is pending may (1) order any party to produce and permit the inspection and coping or photographing, by or on behalf of the moving party, of any designated documents, papers, books, accounts, letters, photographs, objects, or tangible things, not privileged, which constitute or contain evidence relating to any of the matters within the scope of the examination permitted by Rule 26(b) and which are in his possession, custody, or control. . ."

Rule 26(b), incorporated by reference in rule 34 for the purpose of delineating the proper scope of discovery, permits examination:

". . .regarding any matter, not privileged, which is relevant to the subject matter involved in the pending action, whether it relates to the claim or defense of any other party... It is not grounds for objection that the testimony will be inadmissible at the trial if the testimony sought appears reasonably calculated to lead to the discovery of admissible evidence."

The documents sought to be discovered by the present plaintiffs consist of the logs of the U.S.S. Joseph P. Kennedy, Jr. for the day in question; any factual testimony or statements obtained by defendant from witnesses; and medical records of defendant relating to plaintiff Claire Dostal's condition after the accident.

This sort of documentation clearly falls within the quoted rules.

II.

THE UNITED STATES IS SUBJECT
TO THE DISCOVERY RULES.

Discovery may be obtained from the United States. "Rule 26 applies to actions by or against the United States, with a special provision in Rule 37(f) that expenses and attorney's fees are not to be imposed against the United States for refusal to make discovery." 4 *Moore's Federal Practice* (2nd ed., 1966) at pp. 1074-1075. As long as military and diplomatic secrets are not involved, the Government cannot suppress facts in its possession "if a private litigant could not do so," *Moore, op. cit.*, Vol. 4, at p. 1619; *Bank Line v. United States*, 163 F.2d 133 (2nd Cir., 1947); *Royal Exchange Assur. v. McGrath*, 13 F.R.D. 150 (S.D.N.Y., 1952).

Reserving full comment for the defendant's answering papers, it would not appear that military or diplomatic secrets would be involved in this case, arising out of injuries suffered by a civilian paying a peacetime visit to a Naval vessel in American waters.

III.

PLAINTIFFS HAVE SHOWN GOOD CAUSE FOR
THE DISCOVERY OF THE DESIGNATED DOCUMENTS.

In essence, the present plaintiffs request discovery of pertinent factual documentary material, obtained by the Navy from naval witnesses and personnel.[1] Quite obviously, these plaintiffs have no way of obtaining this documentation other than by pre-trial discovery. Naval personnel and

---

[1]The sole exception is the statement a Naval investigator obtained from Plaintiff Claire Dostal (item 5, notice of motion). That item is treated separately, *infra*).

files are, as a matter of course, inaccessible to civilians.

In 4 *Moore's Federal Practice* (2nd ed., 1966), at p. 2478 it is said generally of the requirement that "good cause" be shown for the production of documents:

> "In short, any showing that failure to order production would unduly prejudice the preparation of the party's case, or cause him hardship, or injustice, will, support the order."

In *Royal Exchange Assur. v. McGrath*, 13 F.R.D. 150 (S.D.N.Y., 1952), an action against the Attorney General, as successor to the Alien Property Custodian, to recover seized funds, this Court ordered the production under Rule 34 of factual portions of a report prepared by a Department of Justice investigator. Judge Goddard said in part:

> "It is not disputed by the defendant that the material in the report concerning the loan is relevant. As to good cause, the necessity of production for the preparation of the case, or that it will facilitate proof or progress at the trial, are some of the determinative elements. Gordon v. Pennsylvania R. Co., D.C. 5 F.R.D. 510. The showing here of the relative inaccessibility of the witnesses and the records, the difficulty of determining what occurred between corporations on the European continent during the war and the fact that defendant had opportunities to compile information which could scarcely be matched by the plaintiff combine to establish good cause herein." 131 F.R.D.

at p. 152.

It is submitted that these considerations militate in favor of the documents sought by the present plaintiffs. the Navy, operating through its customary investigative procedures, clearly had "opportunities to compile information" beyond the capacity of plaintiffs. Statements of witnesses and pertinent medical records will facilitate plaintiffs' preparation for trial. The witnesses, and their documents, are inaccessible to the plaintiffs.

There is ample precedent for the requested order. In *Bank Line v. United States*, 76 F.Supp. 801 (S.D.N.Y., 1948), this Court ordered the Government to produce testimony taken before a naval board of inquiry following a collision. In *Royal Exchange Assur. v. McGrath, supra*, the Government was ordered to produce a Department of Justice investigator's report.

Plaintiffs also request discovery of a statement taken by a Naval security investigator from plaintiff Claire Dostal, at the Naval dispensary, shortly after the accident. This Court has consistently permitted a party to discovery his or her statement to the adverse party, its insurer or agent. *Parla v. Matson Navigation Co.*, 28 F.R.D. 348 (S.D.N.Y., 1961); *Chatman v. American Export Lines*, 20 F.R.D. 176, 178 (S.D.N.Y., 1956); *Brown v. New York, New Haven & Hartford R. Co.*, 17 F.R.D. 324, 325 (S.D.N.Y., 1955).

In the <u>Parla</u> case, Judge Palmieri, in ordering discovery of a comparable statement, said:

> "On the other hand, where a statement is taken on or about the time of the accident, while the plaintiff is hospitalized, and long before the institution of suit, there is the danger that defendant may have unfairly extracted damaging admissions. Under the circumstances, allowing pre-trial

disclosure appears to be the better course."
28 F.R.D. at p. 349.

In the *Brown* case, Judge Dawson ordered production of statements taken from all witnesses to an accident, including the plaintiff. His discussion is fully applicable to all branches of the present motion:

"But where the statements sought are ones taken at or about the time of the accident complained, the statements are unique, in that they constitute the immediate impression of the facts. Moreover, as in the instant situation, defendant's employees, who took the statements, were on hand at the time of the happening, and controlled the circumstances surrounding the taking of the statements. In this instance, there can be no duplication by a deposition that relies upon memory, and an allegation of these facts, uncontroverted, is a sufficient showing of good cause. See Karttunen v. Drytrans, Inc., supra.

"If the doctrine of good cause is to be so applied to statements taken from witnesses at the time of the accident, there is ever further reason for the application of a similar rule to statements taken at the time from a plaintiff who was the subject of the physical and emotional involvements that occurred.:
17 F.R.D. at p. 325.

<u>CONCLUSION</u>

THIS COURT SHOULD ENTER AN ORDER DIRECTING
DEFENDANT TO PRODUCE, FOR INSPECTION AND
COPYING BY PLAINTIFFS, THE DOCUMENTS
REFERRED TO IN THE NOTICE OF MOTION

Dated: New York, N.Y.,
June 27, 1967

Respectfully submitted,

HAIGHT, GARDNER, POOR
& HAVENS

Attorneys for Plaintiff
80 Broad Street
New York, N.Y. 10004

CHARLES S. HAIGHT, JR.,
Of Counsel

The U.S.S. J.P. Kennedy, Jr. (DD-850)
Source: United States Naval Institute

XVI.   *History of the Kennedy*

The U.S.S. JOSEPH P. KENNEDY, JR. was named in honor of Lieutenant Joseph Patrick Kennedy, Jr., United States Naval Reserve.

Joseph Patrick Kennedy, Jr., was born in Nantasket, Massachusetts, a son of the Honorable Joseph Patrick Kennedy and Mrs. Rose (Fitzgerald) Kennedy. After attending Choate School, Wallingford, Connecticut, and receiving a Bachelor of Arts degree from Harvard, he served at the American Embassies in London and Paris. He enrolled in the Law School of Harvard University in 1939 and enlisted in the U.S. Naval Reserve, Class V-5, on 24 June 1941. This enlistment was terminated on 15 October 1941 so that he could accept an appointment as Aviation Cadet, U.S. Naval Reserve.

Kennedy completed flight training at the Naval Air Station, Jacksonville, Florida, and was designated Naval Aviator on 10 April 1942. After duty with Transitional Training Squadron, Atlantic, he joined Patrol Squadron 293. In 1943 he was transferred to Bombing Squadron 10, having been promoted to Lieutenant (Junior Grade) on 1 May of that same year. He attained the rank of Lieutenant on 1 July 1944 while on temporary duty with Special Air Unit ONE which had the code name of "Project ANVIL". This project was an effort to utilize drones (pilotless, radio-controlled aircraft) as an attack weapon.

Lieutenant Kennedy volunteered as a pilot for the explosive-laden drone Liberator bomber which could not take off the ground by radio-control. He was joined in this dangerous mission by volunteer co-pilot Lieutenant Wilford J. Willy, USN. They were based at Winfarthing (Fersfield) England where exhaustive tests had been undertaken in preparation for the final mission. A special radio search of the air waves was conducted to make sure that the enemy was not using radio frequencies on which it was proposed to operate the drone. These two brave men would pilot the drone off the ground and stay with it until they were sure that radio-control had been gained by two "mother" planes. They were then to bail out over England while the drone, under control of the "mother" planes, would be guided to the coast of Normandy where its flight would culminate in a crash-dive into the V-2 rocket launching site.

The flight group—two control planes and the drone loaded with 21,170 pounds of high explosives—took off on schedule, 12 August 1944. Routine checking of the radio controls was proceeding satisfactorily when, at 6:20 p.m., the drone exploded with two blasts, timed one second apart. One by one, the factors which might have caused the explosion were studied by investigators, but no final conclusion as to the cause was reached.

Lieutenant Kennedy was reported missing on 12 August 1944 and presumed dead a year and a day later. He was posthumously awarded the Navy Cross "For extraordinary heroism and courage in aerial flight as Pilot of a United States Navy Liberator Bomber on August 12, 1944." The citation further states: "Well knowing the extreme dangers involved and totally unconcerned for his own safety, Lieutenant Kennedy unhesitatingly volunteered to conduct an exceptionally hazardous and special operational mission. Intrepid and daring in his tactics with the unwavering confidence in the vital importance of his task, he willingly risked his life in the supreme measure of service and, by his great personal valor and fortitude in carrying out a perilous undertaking, sustained and enhanced the finest traditions of the United States Naval Service."

The USS JOSEPH P. KENNEDY, JR. (DD-850) was built by the Bethlehem Steel Company, Shipbuilding Division, Quincy, Massachusetts. Her keel was laid 2 April 1945 and she was launched on 26 July 1945, under the sponsorship of Miss Jean Kennedy, sister of Lieutenant Joseph Patrick Kennedy, Jr., USNR. The destroyer was commissioned in the Boston Naval Shipyard on 15 December 1945, with Commander Harry G. Moore, USN, in command.

The KENNEDY shipped out of Boston Harbor on 4 February 1946 for shakedown training while based at Guantanamo Bay, Cuba. On board was Seaman Apprentice Robert Kennedy, V6, USNR, who had volunteered from his NROTC unit at Harvard University in order to have the honor of serving on the destroyer named for his brother.

The ship reached Guantanamo Bay on 8 February 1946. The next seven weeks were filled with such training as night target practice, torpedo tracking exercises, anti-submarine warfare maneuvers with submarine SEA LEOPARD (SS 483), night air attack and cruising exercises, fighter-director exercises, boarding and salvage party drills and shore bombardment runs off Culebra Island.

The destroyer returned to Boston on 7 April 1946 for post-shakedown alterations, then joined Destroyer Division 122, Squadron Twelve, at her home base of Newport, Rhode Island. She visited New York City (16-20 May), then trained men of preformed-ships-crews of the Naval Training Station at Newport, while her own men attended courses of instruction at the Fleet Training Center of that port. She celebrated the Fourth of July by playing host to the public at Bristol, Rhode Island. On 8 October she arrived in Norfolk to join Task Force SIXTY-SIX which included Fleet Admiral Leahy's flagship WISCONSIN (BB 64) and heavy aircraft carrier LEYTE (CV 32). This task force left Norfolk astern on 16 October and set course from the Panama Canal on the 25th for Valparaiso, Chile. The JOSEPH P. KENNEDY, JR. reached the last named port on 1 November and was underway on the 6th, conducting fleet tactics enroute to the Canal Zone.   On the afternoon of 8 November she fell aft of WISCONSIN to pick up Fleet Admiral William Daniel Leahy who debarked at Balboa, Panama Canal Zone, the morning of 11 November 1946. The destroyer transited the canal the next day and set sail from Coco Solo on the 20th, bound with her task force for La Guaria Bay, Venezuela. A searchlight display lit the night of 20 November, and JOSEPH P. KENNEDY, JR. manned her rails on the 25th for review by the President of Venezuela. She put to sea that night for battle practice and independent exercises in waters of Cuba. This duty came to an end on 9 December where she arrived on 14 December 1946 to spend the holiday season.

The KENNEDY conducted intensive anti-submarine warfare exercises in Narragansett Bay from her home base of Newport, and was a unit of the screen around the carrier PHILIPPINE SEA (CV 47) as she cruised down the eastern seaboard for gunnery and flight operations in the Caribbean Sea. She returned to Newport from this cruise on 5 May and was in that port on the 15th when she became flagship of Destroyer Division 102, Squadron Ten, U.S. Atlantic Fleet. After anti-submarine tactics with submarine FINBACK (SS 230), she arrived in New York City on 20 June 1947, mooring off Pougkeepsie for the annual regatta in the Hudson River. She followed this event with a naval reserve officer training cruise from Newport to Argentia, Newfoundland, then arrived in New York Harbor on 26 August preparatory to overhaul in the New York Naval Shipyard. She cleared that port on 3 January 1948 for night steaming exercises off the Virginia Capes and tactics with Squadron Ten out of Guantanamo Bay. Returning to Newport on 6 February, she stood out to see with her squadron on the 9th for operations with the Second Task Fleet off Puerto Rico. On 22 February she departed that training area with a striking force which reached Gibraltar on 1 March for duty with the Sixth Fleet.

The JOSEPH P. KENNEDY, JR. was visited by men of the Royal Hellenic Navy at Corfu, Greece. Other duties took her to the Free Territory of Trieste; Tripoli, Libya; Venice and Naples, Italy; and Toulon, France. She cleared Suda Bay, Crete, on 15 June 1948 and returned to Newport on 26 June for duty which included anti-submarine warfare practice with Navy "blimps" and submarines off the Delaware and Virginia Capes. A reserve training cruise to waters of Cuba and the celebration of Navy Day (27 October) at New York City, was followed by Second Task Fleet exercises including "Operation Barndance" a special problem of submarine search and attack. These maneuvers also involved simulated shore bombardment in cold weather operations extending to the Arctic Circle. She was back to Newport on 21 November 1948 and the remainder of the year was spent in local operating areas.

The destroyer cleared Newport on 10 January 1949 on the first of two battle practice cruises to the Caribbean. The second cruise terminated at Newport on 21 March and was followed by voyage repairs in the Boston Navy Yards (19 April-12 May 1942). She was again underway with the Second Task Fleet for the Caribbean on 23 May and returned to Newport on 4 June. Here on 9 June 1949, she became a flagship of Destroyer Squadron Eighteen, and a unit of Destroyer Division 181. In the following weeks, she conducted division exercises and tactics along the eastern seaboard from New York to the Virginia Capes. She cleared Newport on 23 August and reached Gibraltar on 1 September 1949. The flagship of Destroyer Squadron Eighteen, her operations with the Sixth Fleet included liberty for her men in such ports as Istanbul, Turkey; Athens, Greece; Naples and Venice, Italy. She departed Gibraltar on 17 January 1950 for return to Newport on the 27th.

The KENNEDY entered the Boston Naval Shipyard on 31 January 1950 and was underway on 2 May for operations which found her off the Virginia Capes and in waters of the Caribbean. Sailing from Newport, she embarked naval reserve midshipmen at Norfolk, then put to sea on 24 July for a training cruise which included calls at Halifax, Nova Scotia; New York City; and a rigorous work-out for midshipmen in operating areas of the Guantanamo Bay Naval Base. This cruise terminated at Norfolk on 1 September and was followed by convoy exercises to Bermuda and off Virginia Beach where she engaged in simulated short bombardment to support the landing of troops. On 3 January 1951 she cleared Newport as flagship of Destroyer Squadron Eight, bound for the Pacific. Steaming by way of Pearl Harbor and Midway Atoll, she reached Sasebo, Japan, on 3 February.

The ship loaded stores and ammunition on the midnight of 3 February 1951, then slipped out of Sasebo Harbor into the Sea of Japan. She entered the combat zone off the east coast of Korea and joined units of the Fast Carrier Task Force SEVENTY-SEVEN. With other destroyers she maintained a continuous radar and sonar search around the carrier striking force which steadily pounded enemy targets on the mainland of Korea and gave direct support to United Nations troops on the front lines. She took time out for voyage repairs at Yokosuka (2-5 March 1951) and after hunter-killer training with escort carrier BAIROKO (CVE 115) off the coast of Honshu, rejoined the Fast Carrier Task Force in the Van Dieman Straits on the morning of 18 March 1951. She was back in Sasebo on 4 april for replenishment and on 8 April, sailed to conduct patrolling the Formosa Straits. This duty terminated at Keelung, Formosa, on 20 May and she reached Wonsan ten days later, taking up bombardment station in that harbor.

The KENNEDY left her bombardment station in Wonsan Harbor on 13 June 1951 and joined other units of Destroyer Squadron Eight in Sasebo, Japan. She cleared the last named port on 17 June 1951 on the second leg of a world cruise which found her at Singapore, Malya; Colombo, Ceylon; and Sirah Harbor, Persian Gulf Port of Bahrain Island. She topped off with fuel in Sirah Harbor and got underway on 10 July to transit the Suez Canal. She entered the Mediterranean Sea from Port Said, Egypt, on 20 July 1951. Sailing by way of Naples and Gibraltar, she terminated her world cruise at Newport on 9 August 1951, almost eight months since leaving that home base on 3 January. The remainder of the year was spent in Atlantic Fleet exercises along the eastern seaboard to the Caribbean, and in holiday leave at Newport.

The KENNEDY underwent overhaul in the Boston Naval Shipyard (4 January-20 May 1952), and put to sea from Newport on 28 May to conduct battle practice with her squadron out of Guantanamo Bay. She returned from this cruise to Norfolk on 15 July to serve as a studentship for the Fleet Training School of that base until 4 October. She then resumed training in local areas of Newport until 7 January 1953 when she put to sea for the Mediterranean in company with attack carrier TARAWA (CVA 40) and units of Destroyer Flotilla Six. The task group reached Trieste on 24 January 1953 and the JOSEPH P. KENNEDY, JR. completed her tour of duty with the Sixth Fleet when she left Gibraltar astern on 9 May for return to Newport on the 18th. Voyage repairs in the Boston Naval Shipyard were followed by hunter-killer exercises off the coast of Nova Scotia and a battle practice cruise to the Virgin Islands. On 5 January 1954 she was again underway from Newport for operations in the Mediterranean until 12 May when she cleared Genoa for return to Newport on the 26th. Local tactics were intervened by overhaul in the Philadelphia Naval Shipyard (4 August-8 November 1954). After a refresher training cruise to Guantanamo Bay and serving on plane guard station for the attack carrier BENNINGTON (CVA 20) off Mayport, Florida, she conducted intensive anti-submarine warfare practice along the northeastern seaboard.

On 5 November 1955, The destroyer shipped out of Newport for Arctic maneuvers enroute to Londonderry, Northern Ireland. She was underway from the last named port on 5 December for Oslo, Norway, where on the 8th, she was host to the United States Ambassador and the Commander-in-Chief of the Royal Norwegian Navy. Underway on 12 November, she conducted "Operation SHORTBREAKER" with PERRY (DD 844) enroute to Bremerhaven, Germany. She shifted to Hamburg on 17 December and spent the Christmas Holiday in Greenwich, England. On 3 January 1956 she left Greenwich astern for tactics with the Sixth Fleet in the Mediterranean before return to Newport on 5 March 1956.

The KENNEDY anchored in Annapolis Roads with her Destroyer Squadron Eight on 1 June 1956, joining battleships IOWA (BB 61) and NEW JERSEY (BB 62), cruisers MACON (CA 134) and DES MOINES (CA 132); and ships of Destroyer Squadron Thirty-two. This task force cleared Norfolk on 5 June for midshipmen practice cruise to Stockholm, Sweden, and Portsmouth, England, then to Guantanamo Bay for training maneuvers in the Caribbean before return to Annapolis on 1 August 1956. The destroyer underwent overhaul in the New York Naval Shipyard (14 August-15 November) and departed Newport on 28 January 1957 for a winter schedule out of Guantanamo Bay. On 6 May she got underway from Newport for another tour of duty in the Mediterranean . Her first port of call was Cartagena, Spain, where she arrived on 17 May and was visited by Rear Admiral Castillo, Admiral of the Arsenal of the Spanish Navy; Rear Admiral Bobadillo, Admiral to the Second Division of the Spanish Fleet; the General of the Cartagena Army; and the Mayor of Carteangena. She put to sea on 20 May 1957 for antisubmarine warfare demonstrations with SABLEFISH (SS 303) and in company with the Spanish destroyers SNS IRANDE and SNS ESCANO. This service was followed by training of Naval Academy Midshipmen who were embarked in Barcelona for practice cruising in the Straits of Sicily and the Tyrrhenian Sea where the destroyer joined the attack carrier LAKE CHAMPLAIN (CVA 39) and her tasks group of cruisers and destroyers for "Operation Haystack."

The KENNEDY spent 4 July 1957 in Marseilles, France. After further maneuvers off the coast of Spain she touched at Lisbon, Portugal (17-22 July) on her way back to Newport where she arrived on 1 August. On 3 September she cleared port to rendezvous with a striking force which included the anti-submarine warfare carrier TARAWA (CVS 40) conducting "Exercise Seaspray" enroute to Firth of Clyde, Scotland. In ocean approaches of this port she operated on rescue station for the attack carrier SARATOGA (CVA 60) and took part in operations with the guided missile cruiser BOSTON (CAG 1). On September 17 she departed Firth of Clyde to join in the North Atlantic Treaty Organization "Operation Strikeback" which extended along the coast of Norway. Returning from this cruise to Newport on 22 October, 1957, she spent the holiday season in the Bethlehem Steel Yard, East Boston, Massachusetts. She left that yard on 12 January 1958 for inter-type exercises with attack carriers SARATOGA (CVA 60) and ESSEX (CVA 9) in the North Atlantic and along the eastern seaboard in waters reaching to Bermuda.

The KENNEDY was off Bermuda on 1 February when she pointed her bow for Cannes, France, in company with Destroyer Squadron EIGHT and the attack carrier SARATOGA. The task group reached Cannes on 18 February to join the Sixth Fleet. On 2 April, JOSEPH P. KENNEDY, JR. left Port Said to transit the Suez Canal for a tour of service with the Middle East Forces in the Persian Golf. She re-entered the Mediterranean from Port Said on 7 May and cleared Phelern Bay, Athens, Greece, on 19 June for return to Newport on 1 July 1958, Commander of Destroyer Squadron EIGHT flew his pennant in DECATUR (DD 936) as she took part in convoy exercises along the eastern seaboard to Jacksonville, Florida.

The destroyer entered the Boston Naval Shipyard on 16 December 1958 for overhaul which was complete by 19 March 1959. After a refresher training cruise from Newport to Guantanamo Bay, she became flagship of Destroyer Division 102, Destroyer Squadron Ten, on 12 May 1959. She anchored in Annapolis Roads on 3 June to embark midshipmen for the Inland Sea (The five Great Lakes of the United States) Trailing Cruise. After maneuvers off the Virginia Capes and in Narragansett Bay she cleared Newport on 15 June, bound for the Saint Lawrence Seaway in company with a Task Group of twelve other destroyers led by the frigate WILLIS A. LEE. Also in company were two landing dock ships, a tank landing ship, and fleet submarine CORSAIR. This task group under Rear Admiral E.B. Taylor, represented the United States and her Navy at the Seaway Opening

Lt. Joseph P. Kennedy, Jr.
United States Naval Reserve
25 July 1915 - 12 August 1944

U.S.S. Joseph P. Kennedy, Jr. (DD-850) 1962 -
Courtesy U.S.N.I.

ceremonies held in Montreal, 26 June 1959, wherein Queen Elizabeth and President Eisenhower officially dedicated the Seaway on behalf of the two countries. In the formal opening ceremonies near St. Lambert Lock, near Montreal, President and Mrs. Eisenhower were guests aboard the Royal Yacht BRITANNIA which carried Queen Elizabeth and Prince Philip through the New St. Lawrence Seaway.

At daybreak of 27 June 1959, the JOSEPH P. KENNEDY got underway for transit of the Saint Lawrence Seaway on her way to the very heart of the continent to show the Fleet to the people of the Great Midwest. She passed through the Eisenhower Lock on the morning of 28 June, and that afternoon, entered Lake Ontario from the Iroquois Lock enroute to Chicago. The fourteen naval warships, the first armed men-of-war in the Great Lakes since the War of 1812, reached that port on 2 July for a round of ceremonies preceding the visit of Queen Elizabeth to Chicago on the Fourth of July.

The KENNEDY shifted to Michigan City Harbor, Indiana, on 10 July 1959. In the following weeks she played host to thousands of Midwesterners at Milwaukee, Wisconsin; Detroit, Michigan; and Erie, Pennsylvania. She returned to the Boston Navy Yard on 6 August and resumed operations from Newport which included plane guard duty with the attack aircraft carrier FRANKLIN D. ROOSEVELT (CVA 42) off the Virginia Capes. After overhaul in the Boston Naval Shipyard, she got underway from Newport on 21 March 1960 for the Mediterranean. She reached Gibraltar on 31 March 1960 for barrier patrol duty with attack carriers FORRESTAL and FRANKLIN D. ROOSEVELT out of Naples and Barcelona. She also visited Marseilles and conducted maneuvers off Crete in company with attack carrier INTREPID (CVA 11). On 12 August 1960 her crew was royally entertained in the French Riviera home of Joseph P. Kennedy, father of the Navy hero in whose honor she was named. She cleared Rota, Spain, on 7 October and resumed operations from her home

U.S. Naval destroyer U.S. S. Perry (DD 844) -
Courtesy U.S.N.I.

port of Newport, Rhode Island, on 15 October 1960.[2]

XVIII.   *The Kennedy: 1965-1972*

In early 1965 KENNEDY helped qualify two newly constructed Polaris submarines and went to Boston Naval Shipyard for a three month overhaul. CDR J.W. HAYES, JR. took command of KENNEDY from CAPT J.V. PETERS on July 14, 1965; the next day marked the beginning of a two month period of Refresher Training as the ship set sail for Guantanamo Bay, Cuba. In December 1965 she operated off Bermuda as part of the Recovery Forces for Gemini 7/6.

From February to July 1966 KENNEDY deployed to the Sixth Fleet. Her requirements this time found her in the ports of the eastern Mediterranean and in Malta where she assisted in a dedication of a memorial to the late President. In November, KENNEDY operated as part of the Gemini XII Recovery Forces off Bermuda. December found her operating in the Major AAW/ASW exercises entitled NIANTFLEX 66.

On 1 March 1967 KENNEDY deployed once again to the Sixth Fleet, however, this time the deployment was highlighted by a six week assignment to the Middle East Force. After several operational NATO exercises and visits to the ports of Tunis, Valletta, Malta and Iraklion, Crete, KENNEDY transited the Suez Canal and operated in the Red Sea and Indian Ocean helping to guard U.S. interests in that area.

Due to the Arab-Israeli hostilities which closed the Suez Canal, KENNEDY rounded the Cape of Good Hope on her return trip.

On September of 1967 KENNEDY participated in joint U.S.-Canadian operations and in october she participated in the Apollo IV

------

[2]Navy Department, Office of the Chief of Naval Operations, U.S. Naval Institute.

President John F. Kennedy visits the U.S.
Coast Guard 1962 - Courtesy U.S.N.I.

Recovery operations, manning a secondary recovery area. In November 1967 CDR PETER F. KLEIN relieved CDR J.W. HAYES as Commanding Officer.

In January 1968 KENNEDY deployed to the Caribbean for "Springboard 68". In April 1968, the ship deployed again for the Mediterranean where she participated in a joint NATO exercise in May, and was part of a three day air and sea demonstration commemorating the 20th anniversary of the Sixth Fleet.

During May, June and July, two groups of Naval Academy midshipmen and three foreign officers were assigned to the KENNEDY as part of their training program.

KENNEDY returned to Newport late in September 1968 to prepare for a four month shipyard overhaul which commenced in December. The overhaul provided KENNEDY with the latest improvements in weaponry, communications, and electronic systems.

The overhaul completed late in April, KENNEDY returned to Newport to make preparations for refresher training in Guantanamo Bay, Cuba.

KENNEDY returned to Newport from Guantanamo Bay, Cuba, in late August. In September 1969 CDR T.A. ROGERS relieved CDR P.F. KLEIN as Commanding Officer. The KENNEDY again deployed to the Mediterranean this time from November until May. The KENNEDY visited Malta, Spain, Italy, and Turkey and participated with units of the French Fleet in Anti-Submarine Warfare exercises. The KENNEDY also participated in an officer exchange program, hosting officers from the French, Greek and Turkish Navies.

After some well earned leave for the officers and crew, followed by one month's duty in the Caribbean, the KENNEDY hosted many distinguished U.S. and foreign guests for the 1970 Newport America's Cup Races, won by the defender, INTREPID over the gallant challenge of the

U.S.S. Joseph P. Kennedy, Jr. (DD 850) Navy/68

Australian GRETEL II.

In October 1970 the Kennedy cruised to Bermuda, there participating in a joint U.S./Canadian Anti-Submarine exercise in the North Atlantic. In February of 1971, KENNEDY again engaged in Anti-Submarine workup exercise in preparation for deployment in the Western Atlantic. In March she visited San Juan, Puerto Rico, before returning to Newport.

In February 1972, KENNEDY participated in Operation SNOWY BEACH, an amphibious operation conducted off the northern coast of Maine, in order to determine the effectiveness of the Navy-Marine Corps team under extremely cold weather conditions. KENNEDY sailed to the Carribean in April 1972 to participate in Operation LANTREADEX-72, a high intensity anti-submarine warfare exercise with surface and subsurface units of the U.S. Atlantic Fleet.

On June 13, 1972, KENNEDY left Newport, R.I. with Destroyer Squadron Twenty-Four for her eleventh deployment with the Sixth Fleet in the Mediterranean Sea. During this six month deployment KENNEDY participated in numerous amphibious and anti-submarine warfare exercises with units of the French, Italian, Greek and Turkish navies. KENNEDY also visited the Mediterranean ports of Barcelona, Spain; Naples, Italy; Athens and Corfu, Greece; and the famous Rock of Gibraltar. KENNEDY returned to Newport, R.I. on December 18, 1972, and thus concluded the final Mediterranean deployment in her distinguished 28 year history.[3]

---

[3]Courtesy of the United States Naval Institute, Annapolis, MD.

PART FIVE

The Silence

XVIII   _The Freedom of Information Act_

The case of Dostal vs. The United States of America lasted from 1963 to 1969. Dostal was explicitly told that since the case involved the United States Navy, she would not be able to talk about it; that certain security risks were involved, even though the incident and lawsuit were not involved directly with security matters. The Navy simply did not want this case to go public.

In 1974, the Freedom of Information Act took on a new light regarding the Military:

> "In the wake of Watergate the news media are badgering the public man and branding as 'cover-up!' the slightest suspicion that any scrap of military information is being withheld. In our lemming-like rush to achieve totally 'open' government, we are making it easy for enemy planners and impossible for our own."

The concept of developing national standards for 'freedom of information' without regard for international realities must be examined closely by responsible Americans. No freedom is absolute within civilized societies. Some accommodation must be reached in determining how much information regarding our defense effort is to be placed in the public domain. Supplying complete freedom of information on military matters to the American public would automatically provide the information to our potential enemies as well.

67

Winston Churchill stated at the 1943 Teheran Conference: "In war," he said, "truth is so precious that she should always be attended by a bodyguard of lies."

It has been stated by civilian leaders from the Secretary of Defense to the President that they approved the Cambodian bombing operation as necessary for the protection of American troops.

Under the totally new concept of "open information" on military operations, the actions of our commanders were considered deceitful toward their own country, and the military was pictured in conflict with the best interests of the American people.

This situation has now progressed to the point where the Department of Defense and the military services live in the strange light of inquiry on almost every aspect of our defense efforts. Even attempts to cover operational movements of military units are met with opposition from the press and some members of Congress. This opposition highlights the fallacy of including tactical and strategic deception in the freedom of information program. Under this concept, the U.S. Navy would lie open and exposed. Our opponents would know our every move, and our ships would be continuously pinpointed. Our ability to use the vast breadth of the world's oceans as cover would be ended, and the tactical advantage of mobility virtually lost.

The implications of this growing demand for U.S. military plans, openly arrived at in any developing or future conflict, are readily apparent. In effect, if unchecked, this demand could force us to play in the international "balance of power" arena with our national military thoughts, abilities, and actions completely exposed, while our opponents hide theirs. If continued, we would no longer be able to rely safely on any military course of action other than massive power and head-on assault. This is a doctrine that has proven costly in terms of money, men, and defeat throughout history. It is a doctrine our Navy has neither the men, forces nor weaponry to implement and survive".[4]

Faculty Members study a course agenda in front
of Naval Justice at Newport, R.I. - Courtesy U.S.N.I.

---

[4]Excerpts from: *Military Cover and Deception vs. Freedom of
Information,* by Rear Admiral Wycliffe D. Toole, Jr., United States Navy,
U.S. Naval Institute Proceedings, December 1975.

Dostal's accident on May 3, 1963 occurred 34 years ago. It took two years of research, inquiries, phone calls, and letter writing to obtain the records necessary for this historical document.

Efforts were frequently met with resistence or younger personnel had replaced more experienced colleagues and so often the research went in a circle or wound up in a cul-de-sac.

The initial investigation started at the United States Naval Institute's "Attic Library", Annapolis, Maryland. This library contains older documents, photos, files and books about the United States Navy. Somewhere in a back room a file was produced about the history of the J.P. Kennedy, Jr. With further inquiries about the ship's log, it was learned that this material was held at the Naval Historical Center in Washington, D.C.

David C. Branand
Attorney at Law

January 23, 1997

Ms. Loretta Huntington
Naval Historical Center (DL)
Building 57
Washington Navy Yard
Washington, DC 20347-0571

Dear Ms. Huntington:

This letter is to confirm my secretary's conversation with you on January 6, 1997.

In the conversation she requested a copy of the May 3, 1963 log from the U.S.S. J.P. Kennedy, Jr. (DD850) which was based in New Port, RI at the time.

You kindly indicated that my request would take 3-4 weeks to fulfill.

Thank you for your attention to the above.

Sincerely,

David C. Branand, Esq.

cb:DCB

2/13/97

IN REFERENCE TO   DAVID C. BRANAND
ATTORNEY AT LAW

ENCLOSED IS A COPY OF 3 MAY 1963 DECK LOG
OF THE J.P. KENNEDY, JR. (DD 850)

* * * *

A copy of the log was eventually received in mid-February, 1997.

In January a call was made to one of the attorneys who represented Dostal in the case (Rambush). He said that he would look into the matter regarding those files. By June 1997, Rambush had not responded to the verbal inquiry.

A letter was then written to Rambush as follows:

CLAIRE BRANAND & ASSOCIATES

June 27, 1997

Mr. Leonard K. Rambush, Esquire
Haight, Gardner, Poor & Havens
195 Broadway, Suite 234
New York, New York 10007

Dear Mr. Rambush:

I spoke with either your Secretary or the firm's records management in January of this year, who confirmed that the case of Dostal vs. The United States Navy had not been thrown out, but that it was closed in 1975 and put

72

into storage.

In the beginning of May, I spoke with you directly about my effort to produce a novel about the lawsuit. At that time you offered to have the files retrieved so that I would have accurate references for the book. In the interim, I would like to know the status of this retrieval, if possible.

For your information, I am enclosing the U.S.S. J.P. Kennedy's ships log of May 3, 1963 as well as my outline for the book. I am sorry that I did not know your name when the outline was prepared, but I intend to have this emended in the actual document.

Thank you for your attention to the above.

Best regards,

Claire D. Branand
nee: Dostal

wm:CDB
enc.

With the following reply:

Haight, Gardner, Poor & Havens
195 Broadway • New York 10007 • (212) 341-7000

Lennard K. Rambusch
212/341-7133

July 1, 1997

Dear Ms. Branand:

Thank you for your letter of June 27th.

I have checked with our File Department who advises that the file, which was sent to storage in 1975, was destroyed some years later as a matter of routine.

Accordingly, we are not in a position to provide you with any materials from the file.

Sincerely,

LKR:rl   Lennard K. Rambusch

Starting back to square one, a call was placed to the Records Room at Haight, Gardner, Poor & Havens.

"Was there a case number?"

"Yes."

"Where do I go?"

"Call the Southern District Court of N.Y. City."

The District Court said, "It's in the Archives in N.Y. City."

Call the Archives.

"Do you have a file on case #65 AD 460?" (which means 1965 Admiralty/46th docket)

"Yes."

Call N.Y. Retrieval Service.

Received file on July 9, 1997.

Pre-trial Hearing isn't in file.

* * * * *

CLAIRE BRANAND & ASSOCIATES

TO: Mr. Bruce Lazarus
c/o Legalese
139 Fulton St. Suite 1013
New York, New York 10038

DATE: September 2, 1997

FROM: Claire Branand

#PGS: 1

FAX #:   (212) 393-9796

Per our telephone conversation, I wish to retain your services to retrieve the following file from the National Archives in Manhattan at 201 Varick Street.

CAPTION: DOSTAL vs. THE UNITED STATES NAVY

COURT DOCKET NO.: 65 ADF 460 (Case settled in 1969)

The case was retrieved and confirmed of availability by Rich Gelkbe at the Archives. (212) 337-1300. I understand that your services will cost $45.00 per hour with an estimate of two hours of work, plus $0.50 per page for copies. The file contains approximately 100 pages. Please mail the copy of the file to the above address along with your bill.

Sincerely,

Claire Branand

* * * * *

Call Department of the Navy, Office of Judge Advocate General.

"Please write to Mr. Joe Carter about your inquiry."

* * * * *

CLAIRE BRANAND & ASSOCIATES

August 1997

Mr. Joe Carter
Department of the Navy
Office of the Judge Advocate General
200 Stovall Street, Room 8N45
Alexandria, VA 22332-2400

Dear Mr. Carter

Per your request, I am enclosing as much information that I have regarding a civil lawsuit against the United States Navy which was settled out of court in May, 1969. With this information, I hope that you will be able to retrieve a copy of the pre-trial hearing.

I would like a copy of this hearing for a research project that I am doing.

I hope that the following data will enable you to proceed:

1.   The accident occurred on the U.S.S. J.P. Kennedy, Jr. DD850 on May 3, 1963 (see ship's log attached).

2.   The victim sustained the following injuries: spinal contusions and a fractured coccyx.

3.   The victim's mother filed a civil lawsuit against the United States Government during the summer of 1963.

4.   The law firm which represented the plaintiff was: Haight,

Gardner, Poor & Havens. Mr. Leonard K. Rambush was the attorney of record. The law firm did not keep files beyond 1975.

5. The lawsuit was settled out of court after the pre-trial hearing which was held in New York, N.Y. in the Spring of 1969.

6. The case was captioned: *DOSTAL vs. THE UNITED STATES GOVERNMENT* or *CLARA A. DOSTAL vs. THE UNITED STATES GOVERNMENT.*

Thank you for your attention to the above.

Very Truly,

Claire Branand

* * * * *

CLAIRE BRANAND & ASSOCIATES

September 15, 1997

Mr. Ed Kenny
Department of Justice
Admiralty and Shipping Section
Jacob Javitz Federal Building
26 Federal Plaza Room 320
New York, N.Y. 10278-0140

RE: <u>Dostal vs. The United States of America</u>
Docket No. 65 AD. 460

Dear Mr. Kenny:

Per our conversation of Friday, September 12, 1997, I am enclosing a copy of several documents pertaining to the above captioned case.

These documents were retrieved from the National Archives in manhattan at 201 Varick Street. The file suggests that other pertinent documents are at the Department of Justice.

The Attorneys for the Defendant are listed as:

> Robert M. Morganthau, Esq.
> United States Attorney
> Louis E. Greco, Esq.
> Attorney in Charge
> Admiralty and Shipping Section
> Department of Justice
> New York, New York

The above captioned case was an action pursuant to the Public Vessels Act, 46 U.S.C. Sections 781-790, for personal injuries, property loss, expenses and loss of services arising out of a fall by Plaintiff Claire Dostal from the U.S.S. J.P. Kennedy, Jr. (DD850) on May 3, 1963.

On April 30, 1965, Charles S. Haight, Jr., Esq., who represented the Plaintiff, served a copy of the libel in the above action upon the Honorable Nicholas de B. Katzenbach, Attorney General of the United States.

Defendant's answer was filed and served on February 15, 1967 and a pre-trial conference was held on November 8, 1968. A settlement was made on June 3, 1969.

I would like to confirm the existence of this file at the Department of Justice as I wish to retrieve a copy. The only other number referring to the file is:

Dostal v USA 3591-1

Thank you for your attention to the above.

Sincerely,

Claire Branand nee: Dostal

* * * * *

U.S. DEPARTMENT OF JUSTICE

Re: Dostal v. United States
        Docket No. 65 AD. 460

Dear Ms. Branand:

Your letter of September 15th brings back some memories and nostalgia, despite inability to comply with your request. You see, when I started practicing law in 1966 Louis E. Greco was the attorney in Charge of this office and I interviewed with him and was offered a job in the office (which I did not take at that time but did four years later). Charles S. Haight, Jr. was then an associate at his father's firm, Haight, Gardner, Poor & Havens. Robert Morgenthau later switched to the judicial department of New York City/State and still is a legend there. Charles S. Haight, Jr. in 1976 was appointed to the bench of the United States District Court for the District of New York and has become known as among the best judges in admiralty matters, and otherwise. I joined the office as a Trial Attorney in 1970 and in 1981 became the Attorney in Charge when the office's name was changed to Department of Justice's Civil Division's "New York Field Office of the Torts Branch, Aviation/Admiralty" (some people in D.C. deciding that because airplanes and ships both navigate they belong together in one branch).

Your file, most likely, was shipped to the Federal Records Center circa 1970, where it stayed for about 15 years when it was destroyed (probably part of some land fill in New Jersey). Most likely, a similar fate visited the navy's copy of statements, etc. The only place where you *might* become lucky would be in the court's closed files. Your task will not be that easy,

79

as Docket Numbers like 65 AD 460 (standing for the 460th admiralty case filed in 1965 in the District Court for the Southern District of New York) do not exist any more. Nowadays, the docket numbers show what is and what is not admiralty. You may wish to write to the

Clerk of the Court
U.S. District Court
Southern District of New York
500 Pearl Street
New York, NY 10007

as there may be a way of retrieving documents from the court's dead files, if the statement was filed with the answers to interrogatories, which is a big "if".

As for the disposition of the case, we found one little card notation which indicates that attorney Robert E. Coppola was the last government attorney working on the case. Mr. Coppola now (and since 1970) practices in Long Beach, California. If I am not mistaken, he is a partner at the firm:

Baker & Hostetler
300 Oceangate Ste 620
Long Beach, CA 90802
Office: 310-432-2827
Home tel: 818-790-2516
Fax Nr.: 310-432-6698

This is the best I can do to help you. If you care to let me know, I'd appreciate your advises as to your success or *purpose of inquiry*.

Sincerely,

Janis G. Schulmeisters
Attorney in Charge

When James. H. Webb, Jr. (former Secretary of the Navy, 1987) was invited to write an article for the *Washingtonian* magazine about women entering the United States Naval Academy in 1976, he responded with a realistic point of view entitled *"Women Can't Fight"*.

"...it challenged the growing political sentiment for women in combat roles as well as the presence of women at the service academies." "There is a place for women in our military, but not in combat", he wrote.

In a graphic opening passage he described combat conditions as he and his troops had experienced them in Vietnam. Months without bathing except in muddy communal baths, forced marches laden with seventy pounds of gear, answering calls of nature by straddling a slit trench dug between fighting holes, for security reasons always within sight of other Marines. He told of waking up in the middle of the night to the sounds of one of his machine gunners stabbing a dead soldier, "emptying his fear and frustration into the corpse's chest".

"We killed and bled and suffered and died in a war that Washington society, which seems to view service in the combat arms as something akin to a commute to the Pentagon, will never comprehend," he wrote.

He argued that Congress, in requiring the service academies to admit women, had diluted their mission, which he saw first and foremost as the training of combat leaders, a role for which he insisted women were monumentally ill-suited. Women were a distraction to the men he asserted, "poisoning" their preparation for combat command.

He recounted the trials of his own plebe year, the testing and the abuse, of crying in the closet after the paddling, with the laundry bag over his head.

"That was the plebe system," he wrote. "It was harsh and cruel. It was designed to produce a man who would be able to be an effective

Naval Station, Norfolk, Va.: A woman in the Navy salutes as she reports for duty aboard the submarine tender U.S.S. L.Y. Spear AS-36 - Courtesy U.S.N.I.

Naval Station, Norfolk, Va.: Operations Specialist
Second Class Kelly stands on the bridge of the
repair ship U.S.S. Vulcan AR-5 - Courtesy U.S.N.I.

Norfolk, Va. - Ensign Linda Day reports for duty
aboard the submarine tender U.S.S. L.Y. Pear, AS-36.
She is one of the first groups of female officers to
serve aboard Navy ships - Courtesy U.S.N.I.

James Webb, former Secretary of the Navy at the
123rd Annual Meeting at the U.S. Naval Institute,
Annapolis, MD, 1996 - Courtesy U.S.N.I.

A South Vietnam Liaison Officer off the U.S.
Minesweeper Firm (MSO 444) searches a junk
stopped in Vietnam waters (1965)
Source: U.S. Naval Academy

leader in combat, to endure prisoner-of-war camps, to fight this country's wars with skill and tenacity. And it is all but gone."[5]

adroitly opines the role of women in the military. It is understandable that Dostal, as a female civilian could have fallen off of a destroyer. But to emphasize 's stance, the following mysterious item appeared in a Spring, 1997 *Baltimore Sun* newspaper edition:

WOMEN LOST AT SEA MARS
FEMALE DEBUT ABOARD CARRIER

MAYPORT NAVAL STATION, Fla. — "A female sailor on the U.S.S. John F. Kennedy was lost overboard a day after the aircraft carrier left port with its first contingent of women crew members, the Navy said yesterday.

The ship was 130 miles north-east of its home port near Jacksonville, conducting routine flight operations, when the incident occurred Wednesday, the Navy said.

The woman's name and details of the incident were withheld. Search and rescue operations continued into the night and yesterday."

Perhaps the lifeline hadn't been secured properly.

* * * * *

---

[5]*The Nightengale's Song*, by Robert Timberg © 1995.

Caroline Kennedy Christens USS *John F. Kennedy* (CVA-67).
Courtesy U.S.N.I.

Due to the Freedom of Information Act, Claire Branand was able to retrieve the documents necessary to write her account of *OVERBOARD*.

She thanks the following people and institutions for their assistance:

The United States Naval Institute
Annapolis, MD

U.S. Department of Justice
New York, N.Y.

Naval Historical Center
Washington, D.C.

Bruce Lazarus
Legalese
New York, N.Y.

Rudy Green
Haight, Gardner, Poor & Havens
New York, N.Y.

National Archives
New York, N.Y.

Donald W. Henshaw
Office Doctor, Inc.
Washington, D.C.

U.S. Department of Justice
Office of Information and Privacy
Washington, D.C.

Gen. Perry Hoisington, Ret.
U.S.A.F.
Washington, D.C.

PART SIX

The Conclusion

XXI.   <u>The Pre-Trial Memoranda</u>

The Plaintiff's Pre-Trial Memorandum stated that on May 3, 1963, plaintiff Miss Claire Dostal was a visitor and guest on board the U.S.S. Joseph P. Kennedy, Jr. (DD850), which vessel was then moored outboard the alongside, port side to the U.S. S. Forrest Sherman (DD931) at the U.S. Naval Station, Newport, Rhode Island. Miss Claire Dostal had proceeded on board the U.S.S. Joseph P. Kennedy, Jr at the invitation of Seaman Timothy M. Carmody, a member of the crew of said vessel.

Shortly after proceeding on board the U.S.S. Joseph P. Kennedy, Miss Dostal was caused to fall overboard from the quarterdeck, port side when a lifeline against which she had placed her elbow broke or gave way. Plaintiff fell, striking her back against the side of the U.S.S. Forrest Sherman, and was in the water between these two vessels for a period of at least ten minutes.

The accident and the resulting injuries were caused by the negligence of defendant, its servants, agents and employees, including the officers and crew of the U.S.S. Joseph P. Kennedy, in that they negligently failed to properly maintain and rig the lifeline; negligently failed to warn plaintiff of the hazardous situation and in effect, set a trap for plaintiff by failing to rig the lifeline property; did not have proper appurtenances for rigging the lifeline, and were otherwise reckless and negligent in the premises. The aforesaid conditions existed for a period of time sufficient to warrant the taking of safety precautions. Plaintiff was given no notice or warning of the dangerous hazardous and defective condition. The aforesaid condition constituted a menace, danger, hazard or trap to persons including plaintiff lawfully about the area in which the accident occurred and defendant was further negligent in that it failed to make a proper inspection of the area.

84

Defendant, its agents, servants, employees, officers and crew members were further negligent in the manner in which they maintained, managed, operated and controlled their vessel, including the appurtenances, appliances, installations, gears and areas involved in the accident.

The negligence of the defendant, its agents, servants, employees, officers and crew members as hereinbefore alleged was the proximate cause of injuries to plaintiff as follows: fracture of the coccyx, contusion of the spine, head, thighs, shoulder blades, lower back and left hand; plaintiff was in shock for a period of time after the accident; plaintiff was unconscious at the time she was removed from the water; plaintiff was treated for exposure; plaintiff is presently unmarried but has been advised that as a result of the accident she may experience difficulties during pregnancy and childbirth.

At the time of plaintiff's accident, she was a student and was unable to finish her academic year and was completely disabled through May, 1963, with the resultant loss of $1,500 tuition, which was paid by her parents, also plaintiffs herein. Since the date of her injury, plaintiff has periodically lost time from work, suffers from lower back pain, and is unable to perform or participate in active athletics, dancing, long periods of walking and other normal activities for a person her age. Plaintiff has been advised that her complaints and limitations are permanent in nature.

Plaintiff's working life expectancy at the time of her accident was 46 years.

Plaintiffs' damages are as follows:

(a)	For medical treatment and medications	$1,000.00
(b)	For lost property	300.00
(c)	For loss of school tuition	1,500.00
(d)	For pain and suffering	35,000.00

| (e) | For future pain and suffering | 50,000.00 |
| (f) | For future medical treatment | <u>10,000.00</u> |

Total: $97,800.00

(c) <u>STIPULATED FACTS</u>

1.   That on May 3, plaintiff Claire Dostal was a visitor on board the U.S.S. Joseph P. Kennedy at the invitation of crew member Timothy T. Carmody.

2.   That on May 3, 1963, the U.S.S. Joseph P. Kennedy was owned, operated and controlled by the defendant herein, and was at the U.S. Naval Station, Newport, Rhode Island.

3.   That on May 3, 1963, plaintiff, Claire Dostal, fell from the deck of the U.S.S. Joseph P. Kennedy into the water requiring her rescue by members of the crew of said vessel.

4.   That plaintiff, Clara Dostal, is the mother and plaintiff, Frank Dostal, the father of plaintiff Claire Dostal.

(d) <u>CONTESTED ISSUES OF LAW AND FACT</u>

1.   Defendant's negligence.

2.   Plaintiff Claire Dostal's contributory negligence.

3.   Proximate cause of the accident and the accident's causal relationship to the injuries claimed herein.

4.   Damages.

(e)   AMENDMENT OF THE PLEADINGS: None.

(f)   ISSUES TO BE ABANDONED: None.

(g)   STATEMENT WITH RESPECT TO THE APPLICABLE LAW.

<u>POINT I</u>

DEFENDANT IS LIABLE TO PLAINTIFFS FOR ITS FAILURE TO EXERCISE A HIGH DEGREE OF CARE FOR THE SAFETY OF MISS CLAIRE DOSTAL. <u>Kermarec v. Transatlantique</u>, 358 U.S. 625; Edelman, <u>Maritime Injury and Death</u> (1960).

<u>LIST OF PLAINTIFFS' EXHIBITS</u>

Depending upon the testimony adduced and the exigencies which may arise at the trial of this case, plaintiffs will offer some or all of the following documents and/or parts and portions thereof available at the time:

1.   Hospital and clinical records of the United States Navy, including those of the U.S.S. Joseph P. Kennedy and the Newport Naval Station Medical Facility.

2.   Records relating to examination and/or treatment of plaintiff Claire Dostal since the accident.

3.   Deck Log of the U.S.S. Joseph P. Kennedy.

4.   Investigation conducted by defendant subsequent to the accident to plaintiff and all exhibits appended thereto.

5.   Doctors' bills.

6.   Photographs.

7.   Report of Injury or Poisoning.

8.   Exhibits listed by defendant.

9.   Bills for tuition.

The above is not meant to include such exhibits as may be offered for the purposes of impeachment. Plaintiffs reserve their right to use any other exhibits as may become relevant or as may come to light up to and including the trial of this action.

(h)   <u>PLAINTIFFS' WITNESSES</u>

Depending upon what testimony is adduced at the trial of this case, plaintiffs will produce some or all of the following witnesses and such other witnesses as may be required:

1.   Claire Dostal
2.   Clara Dostal
3.   Frank Dostal
4.   Timothy M. Carmody
5.   Mary Ann Jones
6.   Navy doctor and hospital corpsmen who examined.
7.   Master, officers and crew members of the U.S.S. Joseph P. Kennedy as well as all persons named in defendant's answers to plaintiff's interrogatories.
8.   John Aluza
9.   Dr. Wyman
10.   Dr. LaMotte
11.   Dr. Irving Glick
12.   Dr. Greeley
13.   Dr. Guthrie
14.   Dr. Walter Thompson
15.   Dr. Silverstein
16.   A maritime expert to be designated at a later date.

Plaintiffs reserve the right to call any of the witnesses listed by defendant, and further reserve its right to amend their list of witnesses up to and including the date of trial.

Respectfully submitted,

HAIGHT, GARDNER, POOR & HAVENS
Attorneys for Plaintiffs

* * * * *

The Defendant's Pre-Trial Memorandum was filed with the U.S. District Court in New York on November 21, 1968 by Robert M. Morgenthau, U.S. Attorney for the Department of Justice.

The statement of the Government Position was that:

The defendant, United States of America, contends that if the plaintiff, Claire Dostal, was injured at the time and under the circumstances as alleged in the complaint, which is denied, the injuries were not caused or contributed to by any defect in the vessel or its equipment; that any injuries sustained by plaintiff were caused solely by her contributory negligence.

Undisputed Facts

(1)   At all times mentioned in the complaint, the United States of America was the owner of the U.S.S. Joseph P. Kennedy, Jr.

(2)   At all times mentioned in the complaint, the United States of America operated and was in control and possession of the U.S.S. JOSEPH P. KENNEDY, JR.

(3)   On or about May 3, 1963, the U.S.S. JOSEPH P. KENNEDY, JR. was moored in the navigable waters of Narragansett Bay, at the U.S. Naval Station, Newport, Rhode Island.

89

(i)   The plaintiff was negligent in the following respects, among others, which will be proved at the trial of this suit.

The plaintiff, Claire Dostal, was negligent, careless and inattentive in leaning against the vessel's lifeline.

(c)   <u>Disputed Facts</u>

(1)   The general facts and circumstances resulting in the injury to plaintiff.

(2)   Was plaintiff's injury caused by a defect in the ship or appurtenant equipment?

(3)   Was the vessel unseaworthy?

(4)   Was plaintiff's injury caused by the act or acts of employees of the Government?

(5)   Was the plaintiff negligent?

(6)   The nature and extent of plaintiff's alleged injury.

(7)   The amount of plaintiffs' damages, if any.

(d)   <u>Amendments to Pleadings</u>

None.

(e)   <u>Issues Abandoned</u>

None of the issues tendered in the pleadings are abandoned.

(f)   <u>Applicable Law</u>

(1)   Plaintiffs have the burden of proving all elements of their

case, including the alleged negligence of defendant, unseaworthiness, causation, and the nature and extent of their injuries and damages. <u>Selby v. United States</u>, 264 F.2d 632 (2d. Cir. 1959), cert. den. 361 U.S. 815 (1959); <u>Freitas v. Pacific-Atlantic Steamship Co.</u>, 218 F.2d 562 (9th Cir. 1955).

(2)   The maritime doctrine of seaworthiness does not require perfection on the part of the shipowner, but merely that the ship and its appurtenances be reasonably fit for their intended use. <u>Mitchell v. Trawler Racer, Inc.</u>, 362 U.S. 539, 550 (1960); <u>Morales v. City of Galveston</u>, 370 U.S. 165 (1962).

(3)   The warranty of seaworthiness does not extend to a social visitor to a ship not on board to perform ship's work. <u>Kermarec v. Compagnie General Transatlantique</u>, 358 U.S. 625, 629 (1959).

(g)   <u>Government's Exhibits</u>

The following exhibits may be presented at the trial and the Government reserves the right to produce any others necessary to prove its case and to refute issues which may arise at the time of trial.

(1)   Vessel's logs including vessel's medical log and deck log.

(2)   Deposition of plaintiff, Claire Dostal.

(3)   Income tax returns.

(4)   Medical records and x-rays.

(5)   Deck plan of the U.S.S. Joseph P. Kennedy.

(6)   Photographs of the alleged accident area.

(7)   Diagrams and sketches of the alleged accident area.

(8)   Transcripts of plaintiff, Claire Dostal's college and school

records.

       (9)   Letter of Clara Dostal dated July 29, 1963.

       (h)   <u>Government's Witnesses</u>

The following may be presented at the time of trial and the Government reserves the right to present any other witnesses who may be necessary in rebuttal and further reserves the right to call any of the witnesses listed by plaintiff.

      (1)   Richard J. Costa
      (2)   Roger Loren Allen

      (3)   Marvin F. Bringhurst
      (4)   Dr. William Martin
      (5)   Dr. S.L. Green
      (6)   Dr. John A. Arness
      (7)   John L. Rodericks
      (8)   Presently unnamed Government doctor.
      (9)   A maritime expert to be designated at a later date.

All or some of the witnesses may be presented by deposition.

      Respectfully submitted,

      ROBERT M. MORGENTHAU
      United States Attorney
      U.S. Department of Justice

XXII.   <u>The Settlement</u>

On June 3,1969, the United States District Court, Southern District of New York, issued the following satisfaction of judgment:

WHEREAS, a consent judgment was entered in the above-entitled action on April 11, 1969 in favor of plaintiffs Claire Dostal, Clara Dostal, and Frank Dostal, and against defendant United States of America, in the sum of $13,500.00, without interest and costs; and

WHEREAS said judgment has been wholly paid;

THEREFORE, satisfaction of said judgment is hereby acknowledged and the Clerk of this Court is hereby authorized and directed to cancel, satisfy and discharge the same.

XXIII. <u>Sources</u>

U.S. Department of the Navy
Naval Historical Center
Washington, D.C.

U.S. Army
Missile Command Center

U.S. Naval Institute
Archives Library
Annapolis, MD

U.S. Department of Justice
Admiralty and Shipping Section
New York, NY

Robert W. Love, Jr.
History of the U.S. Navy
Volume Two: 1942-1991

Funk & Wagnalls
New Encyclopedia
Funk & Wagnalls, Inc.

Sanford H. Kadish
Monrad G. Paulsen
Criminal Law and its Processes

Peter Johnson
Sail Magazine Book of Sailing

Rosenfeld Photo Collection
Mystic Seaport Museum

The Cuban Crisis: A Documentary Record
Headline Series NO. 157

Admiral R.A. Hopwood
The Laws of the Navy
The Royal Navy

Admiral Wycliffe D. Toole, Jr.
Military Cover and Deception vs. Freedom of Information
U.S. Naval Institute Proceedings

Robert Timberg
The Nightengale's Song

NASA
National Aeronautic and Space Administration

PART VII

The Department of Justice File

BRANAND & ASSOCIATES

December 5, 1997

James Kovakas
Department of Justice
Freedom of Information Unit
901 E Street NW
Washington, DC 20530

      RE: <u>Civil Action 65 AD 460</u>

Dear Mr. Kovakas:

I have been referred to you by Bernard Berglind from the Department of Justice Records Department.

I would like permission to obtain a copy of the above captioned file. Specifically, I would like copies of:

1. All depositions
2. All interrogatories
3. All statements
4. The pre-trial hearing
5. Any other pertinent documents.

I would like the above information in order to include it in a book that I am writing about that case.

Thank you for your attention to the above.

              Very Truly,

              Claire Branand
wm:CDB   Nee: Dostal

U.S. Department of Justice

JMK:JK:145-FOI-3927

February 3, 1998

Ms. Claire Branand
Branand & Associates

Dear Ms. Branand:

This letter is in response to your December 5, 1997 request for documents pertaining to the Civil Division's file relating to Civil Action Number 65 Ad 460.

Pursuant to your request, we conducted a search of the Civil Division's case file system of records and identified reference to the case <u>USS Joseph P. Kennedy, Jr., Claire Dostal, et al. v. US</u>, No. 65 Ad. 460 (S.D.N.Y.). We obtained our file of this case and reviewed the contents under the provisions of the Privacy Act (PA), 5 U.S.C. §552, and the Freedom of Information Act, 5 U.S.C. §552.

Our file contains 174 pages of documents. I determined that 162 pages of documents may be released to you under the PA and the FOIA. Copies of these documents are enclosed.

The remaining twelve pages consist of a six-page Memorandum dated February 6, 1969 and a file copy of this memorandum. This memorandum contains the Civil Division's attorney's analysis of the case and recommendation to his superior, Mr. Lawrence F. Ledebur, Chief, Admiralty and Shipping Section, regarding the proposed settlement of this case. Accordingly, the memorandum is exempt from disclosure pursuant to the PA, 5 U. S. C. §552a(d)(5) which states: "nothing in this section shall allow an individual access to any information compiled in reasonable anticipation of a civil action or proceeding."

I reviewed this memorandum under the provisions of the FOIA and determined that it is an internal Civil Division memorandum exempt pursuant 5 U.S.C. §552(b)(5). This exemption protects those inter-agency or intra-agency communications which are traditionally privileged in civil discovery. Specifically, the memorandum contains the attorney's discussion of legal issues and his recommendation regarding the action to be taken by the Department of Justice with regard to the settlement of this action. The document is exempt pursuant to 5 U.S. C. §552(b)(5) based upon the work product privilege incorporated within this exemption.

If you disagree with my decision to withhold the document responsive to your request as outlined above, you may appeal by writing within 30 working days of the receipt of this letter to the Office of Information & Privacy, Suite 570 FLAG Bldg., United States Department of Justice, Washington, D.C. 20530. Both the letter appealing the decision and the envelope should be clearly marked "FOIA APPEAL". Thereafter, judicial review would be available in the U.S. District Court in the district in which you reside or have your principal place of business or in the U.S. District Court for the District of Columbia.

Sincerely,

James M. Kovakas
Attorney In Charge
FOI/PA Office, Civil Division

Enclosures: 162

BRANAND & ASSOCIATES

February 5, 1998
Richard Huff, Co-Director
Office of Information & Privacy
Suite 750 FLAG Bldg.
United States Department Of Justice
Washington, DC 20530

"FOIA APPEAL"

      RE: <u>Department of Justice Civil Division File # 61-51-4408</u>

Dear Mr. Huff:

I retrieved 162 pages of the above captioned file. Mr. James Kovakas, Attorney In Charge of the FOI/PA Office, Civil Division, has determined that 12 additional pages are exempt from disclosure pursuant to the PA, 5 U.S.C. 552a(d)(5) which states: "nothing in this section shall allow an individual access to any information compiled in reasonable anticipation of a civil action or proceeding." (See attached correspondence).

I wish to appeal that decision. Please advise me of the appropriate process to do so.

                Sincerely,

                Claire Branand
                nee: Dostal

wm:CDB
enc.

100

U.S. Department of Justice
Office of Information and Privacy

February 19, 1998

Ms. Claire Branand

Re: Request No. 145-POI-3927

Dear Ms. Branand:

This is to advise you that your administrative appeal from the action of the Civil Division on your request for information from the files of the Department of Justice was received by this Office on February 10, 1998.

The office of Information and Privacy, which has the responsibility of adjudicating such appeals, has a substantial backlog of pending appeals received prior to yours. In an attempt to afford each appellant equal and impartial treatment, we have adopted a general practice of assigning appeals in the approximate order of receipt. Your appeal has been assigned number **98-1480**. Please mention this number in any future correspondence to this Office regarding this matter.

We will notify you of the decision on your appeal as soon as we can. The necessity of this delay is regretted and your continuing courtesy is appreciated.

Sincerely,

Drema A. Hanshaw
Paralegal Specialist

U.S. Department of Justice

Office of Information and Privacy

September 10, 1998

Ms. Claire Branand

Re: Appeal No. 98-1480
        RLH:TSW:KMF

Dear Ms. Branand:

You appealed from the action of the Civil Division on your request for access to records pertaining to Civil Action No. 65 Ad 460.

As a result of discussions between Civil Division personnel and members of my staff, a supplemental release of six pages is enclosed. Inasmuch as this action constitutes a full grant of your request, I am closing your appeal file in this Office.

Sincerely,

Richard L. Huff
Co-Director

Enclosure

Form No. CV-30
(Rev.12-26-63)

UNITED STATES DEPARTMENT OF JUSTICE
WASHINGTON, D.C.   dms

May 6, 1965

Address Reply to the
Division Indicated
and Refer to Initials and Number
JWD:RL
61-51-4408

Department of the Navy
Washington,. D.C. 20350
        Attention: Admiralty Counsel

Re: USS JOSEPH P. KENNEDY, JR., (DD-850)
        Visitor's injury - May 3, 1963
        Clara Dostal et al. v. United States
        <u>Southern New York - 65 AD 460</u>
        Filed April 30, 1965; Received May 3, 1965

Dear Sirs:

Herewith are copies of a libel or complaint and summons apparently filed with the clerk, and received by us as indicated above. For the defense of this action please send us a report in duplicate of the facts with a list of witnesses and relevant citations to the U. S. Code and Code of Federal Regulations.

Because courts are increasingly reluctant to extend time to answer, we must have a report within 30 days. If a complete report cannot be made within that time, please send us all the information possible and explain the reasons for delay so that we can promptly inform the court.

By a copy of this letter we are advising the United States Attorney of our action in this matter which has been assigned to the admiralty staff attorney whose name and telephone extension appear below.

Yours very truly,

Copies to:
Department of Justice
Admiralty Section
42 Broadway, Room 600
New York 10004

Staff: Mr. Ronald Lovitt, Code 187 ext. 3364

ELW,Jr:ABC:jmf
61-51-4408 LFL
NY 67-200

                    Commissioner
                    Internal Revenue Service
                    Washington, D.C. 20224

                    Re: USS JOSEPH P. KENNEDY, JR.
                    Visitor's Injury, May 3, 1963
                              Claire Dostal, et al. v. United States
                              Southern New York -- 65 Ad. 460

Dear Sir:

        Pursuant to Section 301.6103(a)-I(h), Title 26 CFR, it is
requested that this office be furnished copies of the income tax returns
for the years 1964-1967 inclusive, together with any and all other
information collected by your revenue and intelligence agents
pertaining to Claire Dostal. Miss Dostal's last residence is listed as
137 East 36th Street, New York, New York. Her Social Security
number is 000-00-0000. Please certify these documents for
introduction in evidence.

        This office is defending the interests of the United States in
an action brought by Claire Dostal for injuries allegedly suffered
aboard the USS JOSEPH P. KENNEDY, JR.

        Documents furnished in response to this request will be
limited in use to the purpose for which they are requested and will
under no condition be made public except to the extent that publicity
necessarily results if they are used in litigation.

        Access to these documents on need-to-know basis, will be

limited to those attorneys or employees of my office who are actively engaged in the investigation or subsequent litigation, or other Federal employees assisting me in the investigation. Persons having access to these documents will be cautioned as to the confidentiality of the information contained therein and of the penalty provisions of Section 7213 of the Internal Revenue Code and Section 1905, Title 18, U.S.C. regarding the unauthorized disclosure of such information.

Please send the requested returns or advice with respect thereto to Louis E. Greco, Attorney in Charge, New York Office, Admiralty and Shipping Section, Department of Justice, Room 600, 42 Broadway, New York, New York 10004.

I would appreciate it if you would send a copy of your letter of transmittal to the Chief, Admiralty and Shipping Section, Department of Justice, Washington, D.C. 20530.

Sincerely,

EDWIN L. WEISL, JR.
Assistant Attorney General
Civil Division

U.S. DEPARTMENT OF JUSTICE

LEG::BRC:nw
61-51-4408 RL
(NY 67-104)

February 16, 1967

Commandant
3rd Naval District
90 Church Street
New York, N.Y. 10007

Attention: <u>District Legal Officer</u>

Re: <u>USS JOSEPH P. KENNEDY, JR.</u> -
Visitor's
  Injury, May 3, 1963
Claire Dostal, by Clara Dostal, Clara
  Dostal and Frank Dostal v. United States
<u>SDNY   65 Ad. 460</u>

Dear Sir:

In accordance with Commander Bates' request please find attached a copy of the government's answer filed in this case.

This will confirm our understanding that settlement negotiations will continue between the Department of the Navy and plaintiff's attorney. Mr. Charles S. Haight, Jr. counsel for plaintiff, requested that his settlement negotiations with the Navy Department continue. In the event of a breakdown of negotiations, please advise

107

us at an early date in order that we may take the necessary action to protect the interests of the government.

Very truly yours,

BAREFOOT SANDERS
Assistant Attorney General
Civil Division

By
Louis E. Greco
Attorney in Charge
Admiralty and Shipping Section

LEG:ADG:nw
61-51-4400 RL
(NY 65-104)

September 20, 1967

Department of the Navy
Office of the Judge Advocate General
Washington, D.C. 20350

Attention: <u>Admiralty Counsel</u>

Re: USS JOSEPH P. KENNEDY, JR.
        Visitor's Injury, May 3, 1963
            Claire Dostal, et al. v. United States
            <u>SDNY   65 Ad. 460</u>

Dear Sirs:

This office is defending the interests of the United States in the above captioned litigation.

Plaintiff allegedly sustained injuries on May 3, 1963 when she fell into the water while visiting the USS JOSEPH P. KENNEDY, JR. at Newport, Rhode Island. As you are aware, a protective libel was filed by plaintiff's attorney on April 30, 1965 pending settlement discussions with the Navy. Those discussions have been discontinued and the matter is now being handled by this office.

Interrogatories have been served upon the United States by plaintiff's attorney. The larger part of the information needed to answer these interrogatories is available to us from the Navy's file on this case which was forwarded to us by the District Legal Officer for the Commandant Third naval District. Further information is, however, needed.

Please provide us with the following documents and information for use in the defense of this case:

1. Applicable smooth and rough deck logs covering the date of the accident, May 3, 1963.

2. The applicable quartermaster's notebook covering the date of the accident, May 3, 1963.

3. The vessel's daily medical Journal covering the date of the accident, May 3, 1963.

4. The security log for the U.S. Naval Station, Newport, R.I. covering the date of the accident on May 3, 1963.

5. The injury report made at the Naval Dispensary, U.S. Naval Station, Newport, R.I. regarding plaintiff's injury and the treatment given to her.

6. The injury report made at the U.S. Naval Hospital, Newport, R.I. as to plaintiff's injury.

7. The consultation report made by Dr. W.W. Martin, LT (jg), USNR at the U.S Naval Hospital, Newport, R.I. regarding the injury and treatment of plaintiff after the accident.

8. We note in reviewing the Navy's report of investigation on this accident (LCDR) William J. Longhi, USN. investigative report of May, 29, 1963

forwarded to the Judge Advocate General by the Commandant, First Naval District's third endorsement letter serial 1027ND1-22 of June 27, 1963) that x-rays were taken of plaintiff after the accident at the U.S. Naval Hospital, Newport, R.I.   Information is requested as to the location and identity of the persons in possession of those x-rays.

9.   Enclosures 19 and 20 to the Navy's report of investigation on this accident are photographs of the accident area and of the hook on the stanchion around which the lifeline was attached.   Information, if available at this late date is requested as to the identity of the person who took these photos and as to the date they were taken.

10.   An appropriate deck plan for the vessel covering the area of the accident and reflecting the location of the stanchions supporting the lifeline on May 3, 1963 is needed.   Information is also requested as to the distance between the stanchions and the height above the dock of the lifeline in the area of the accident.

11.   Information is requested as to the present or last known address of the persons set out in the attached list. The command or unit indicated below each name is according to the Navy's report of investigation the one to which the individual was attached at the time of the accident.

Your cooperation is appreciated.

Very truly yours,
CARL EARDLEY
Acting Assistant Attorney General
Civil Division

By

Louis E. Greco
Attorney in Charge
Admiralty and Shipping Section

1.	Dr. W.W. Martin
	LT. (jc) File number unknown
	U.S. Naval Hospital, Newport, R.I.

2.	Dr. J.A. Arness
	LT (jc) File number unknown
	U.S. Naval Dispensary, Newport, R.I.

3.	Nicholas Mikhalevsky
	Commanding officer, rank and file number unknown
	USS JOSEPH P. KENNEDY, JR. (DD 850)

4.	James B. Rucker
	LT. (Jc) File number unknown
	USS JOSEPH P. KENNEDY, JR. (DD 850).

5.	William J. Longhi
	LCDR, USN 512308/1100
	USS JOSEPH P. KENNEDY, JR. (DD 850)

6.	Timothy M. Carmody
	SMSN, 5430385, USN
	USS JOSEPH P. KENNEDY, JR. (DD 850)

7.	Richard J. Costa
	SN, Service number unknown, USN
	USS JOSEPH P. KENNEDY, JR. (DD 850)

8.	Marvin F. Bringhurst
	SM 3, service number unknown
	USS JOSEPH P. KENNEDY, JR. (DD 850)

9.	Roger Loren Allen

BMSN, 541 6271, UNS

10.   William M. Paladechuck
        BM1, service number unknown, USN
        USS JOSEPH P. KENNEDY, JR. (DD 850)

11.   Donald E. Vander Woude
        1C 1, service number unknown
        USS JOSEPH P. KENNEDY, JR. (DD 850)

12.   John L. Rodericks
        BMSN, service number unknown
        USS JOSEPH P. KENNEDY, JR. (DD 850)

13   D.P. Yonkers
        BM2, service number unknown
        USS JOSEPH P. KENNEDY, JR. (DD 850)

14.   F.G. Pitts
        HN, service number unknown
        U.S. Naval Dispensary, Newport, R.I.

DEPARTMENT OF THE NAVY
OFFICE OF THE JUDGE ADVOCATE GENERAL
WASHINGTON, D.C. 20370

17 January 1968

Admiralty and Shipping Section
U.S. Department of Justice
42 Broadway, Room 600
New York, New York 10004

Attn: Mr. A. D. Christian

> Re: USS JOSEPH P. KENNEDY, JR. - Visitor's
> Injury - 3 May 1963 - Claire D. Dostal
> v. United States, S.D.N.Y. 65 Ad. 460
> Your File: (NY 65-104)

Gentlemen:

Please find enclosed a copy of Commanding Officer USS JOSEPH P. KENNEDY, JR., letter Serial 8-68 of 9 January 1968, with the two original enclosures thereto. When the Daily Journal Record has served its purpose, its return by registered mail is requested.

It appears from the Commanding Officer's letter that the quartermaster's notebook has been destroyed, and that the identity of the photographer has not been ascertained. We shall attempt to ascertain the identity of this photographer by other means, if possible.

Sincerely yours,

C. A. BLOCKER
Admiralty Counsel

Copy to:
ADM & SHPG EEC, BJ, Wash CO. USS J.P. KENNEDY, JR.

115

LEG:SDC:md
61-51-4408-RL
(NY 65-104)

U.S. DEPARTMENT OF JUSTICE

January 30, 1968

Haight, Gardner, Poor & Havens, Esqs.
80 Broad Street
New York, New York 10004

Attn: Charles S. Haight, Jr., Esq.

Re: USS JOSEPH P. KENNEDY, JR.
Visitor's Injury - 3 May 1963
Claire D. Dostal v. United States
SDNY 65 Ad. 460

Dear Sirs:

This refers to your letter of January 25, 1968 and will confirm the presentation of Miss Dostal for examination in our office at 3:00 p.m. on Wednesday, February 14, 1968.

Yours very truly,

EDWIN L. WEISL, JR.
Assistant Attorney General
Civil Division
By

Louis E. Greco
Attorney in Charge
Admiralty and Shipping Section

U.S. DEPARTMENT OF JUSTICE

LEG:ADC:aw
61-51-4408-RL
(NY 65-104)

March 14, 1968

Haight, Gardner, Poor & Havens, Esqs.
80 Broad Street
New York, New York 10004

      Attn: <u>Charles S. Haight, Jr., Esq.</u>

      Re: USS JOSEPH P. KENNEDY, JR.
             Visitor's Injury - 3 May 1963
             Claire D. Dostal v. United States
             <u>SDNY 65 Ad. 460</u>

Dear Sirs:

Enclosed are the original and one copy of the deposition of your client Claire Dostal taken on February 21, 1968.

Please have Miss Dostal note any corrections and sign the original before a notary public, returning same to us. The copy is provided for your use.

Yours very truly,

                    EDWIN L. WEISL, JR.
                    Assistant Attorney General
                    Civil Division

                    By

                    Louis E. Greco
                      Attorney in Charge
                      Admiralty and Shipping Section

Encl.

117

Copy From
ADMIRALTY AND SHIPPING SECTION
U.S. Department of Justice
42 Broadway, Room 600
New York 4, N.Y.

LEG:ADC:aw
61-51-4408-RL
(NY 65-104)

April 9, 1968

Department of the Navy
Office of the Judge Advocate General
Washington, D. C. 20370

<u>Attn: Admiralty Counsel</u>

Re: USS JOSEPH P. KENNEDY, JR. - Visitor's
       Injury, May 3, 1963
       Claire D. Dostal v. United States
       <u>SDNY   65 Ad. 460</u>

Dear Sirs:

We refer to our letter of September 20, 1967, requesting various documents and information for use in the above-captioned case and to subsequent correspondence pertaining to this matter.

Your letter, Serial 9889, of October 27, 1967, advised that the injury and consultation reports made at the naval Station Dispensary and Base Hospital were being retrieved from the Records Center. Have these records been retrieved and are they available?

118

You also advised that x-rays of Miss Dostal were being retained at the naval Hospital, Newport. Please obtain these x-rays for us so that we may use them in connection with the physical examination of Miss Dostal by the Government's doctor. In addition, we note that part of the original statement of Miss Claire Dostal (Enclosure 8 to report of investigation) forwarded with your letter was not received by us. Lieutenant Babe Marsh of your office advised in a subsequent telephone conversation with Mr. Christian that the missing portion had not been contained in the original documents forwarded to us and that a check would be made for it. Please advise us as to whether the missing pages have been located.

We were advised by your letter, Serial 10247, of November 7, 1967, that the original of Dr. Green's examination report would be sent to us when received. Please send us the original of this report or advise us as to where it may be located.

Your letter, Serial 504, of January 17, 1968, indicated that an attempt would be made to ascertain the identity of the photographer by other means. Information as to whether your efforts have been successful or your advice in this regard would be useful.

Finally, we would also like to obtain an appropriate deck plan or diagram of the vessel reflecting the area of the accident from an overhead position. The diagram forwarded with the vessel's letter, Serial 8-68, of January 9, 1968, reflects a view from the side looking at the concerned area.

Your assistance in this matter is appreciated.

Yours very truly,

EDWIN L. WEISL, JR.
Assistant Attorney General
Civil Division

By

Louis E. Greco
Attorney in Charge
Admiralty and Shipping Section

US Treasury Department
Internal Revenue Service
Washington, DC 20224
Date: In reply refer to:
April 19, 1968
CP:C:D

Honorable Edwin L. Weisl, Jr.
Assistant Attorney General
Civil Division
Department of Justice
Washington, D.C. 20530

Dear Mr. Weisl:

In re: USS JOSEPH P. KENNEDY, JR.
Visitor's Injury - May 3, 1963
Claire D. Dostal, et al. v. United States
Southern New York - 65 Ad. 460
Symbols: ELW,Jr:ADC:jmf
61-51-4941 LFL
NY 67-200

This refers to your letter of April 8, 1968, requesting copies of the income tax returns of Claire Dostal, 137 East 36th Street, New York, New York, for the years 1964 through 1967, inclusive.

We have asked Mr. Edward J. Fitzgerald, Jr., District Director, Internal Revenue Service, 120 Church Street, New York, New York, to prepare certified copies of the returns and related documents and send them to Mr. Louis E. Greco, Attorney in Charge, New York Office, Admiralty and Shipping Section, Department of Justice, Room 600, 42 Broadway, New York, New York 10004. If copies cannot be furnished for any reason, the District Director will so advise Mr. Greco.

121

Income tax returns for 1967 will not be available for copy purposes for several months. If you wish to renew your request sometime later for the 1967 return of the person named in your letter, we will be glad to consider it.

If we can be of further assistance, please let us know.

Very truly yours,

D.W. Bacon
Assistance Commissioner
(Compliance)

ADMIRALTY AND SHIPPING SECTION
U.S. Department of Justice

LEG:ADC:aw
61-51-4408-RL
(NY 65-104)

May 1, 1968

Department of the Navy
Office of the Judge Advocate General
Washington, D. C. 20370

Attn: <u>Admiralty Counsel</u>

Re: USS JOSEPH P. KENNEDY, JR.
     Visitor's Injury, May 3, 1963
     Claire D. Dostal, et al. v. United States
     SDNY   65 Ad. 460

Dear Sirs:

We refer to your letter of April 9, 1968 and subsequent telephone conversation of April 30, 1968 between Commander Bates and Mr. Christian in the above captioned case.

It is requested that we be furnished an appropriate diagram of the vessel's main deck and the area of the accident reflecting an overhead view. The diagram should, if possible, show the following:

1. Relative position of the brow at the time of the accident to the bow and stern of the vessel.

123

2.   The area on the main deck in the vicinity of the brow reflecting the following:

      a.   Any interferences or obstructions in the area such as deck gear of machinery.

      b.   Size of open area on the Quarterdeck including location and width of any passageways leading off quarterdeck and distances between life line (vessel's edge) and nearest compartment bulkhead.

Your assistance in this matter is appreciated.

Yours very truly,

EDWIN L. WEISL, JR.
Assistant Attorney General
Civil Division

By

Louis E. Greco
Attorney in Charge
Admiralty and Shipping Section

DEPARTMENT OF THE NAVY
OFFICE OF THE JUDGE ADVOCATE GENERAL
WASHINGTON. D.C. 20370

IN REPLY REFER TO JAG:11:GPS:jat
Ser 1265

9 May 1968

From: Judge Advocate General
To: Commanding Officer, USS JOSEPH P. KENNEDY JR
            (DD 850)

Subj: USS JOSEPH P. KENNEDY, JR. - Visitor's Injury -
            3 May 1963 -
            Claire Dostal v. United States, S.D.N.Y. 65 Ad. 460

1.   In connection with the defense of subject matter, the
Department of Justice has requested a diagram of the area of
the main deck where the accident occurred from an overhead
view. Please furnish us with a diagram illustrating the:

        a.   Relative position of the brow at the time of the accident
to the bow and stern of the vessel.

        b.   The area on the main deck in the vicinity of the brow
reflecting the following:

                (1)   Any interferences or obstructions in the area
                        such as deck gear or machinery.

                (2)   Size of open area on the Quarterdeck including
                        location and width of any passageways leading

125

off quarterdeck and distances between life line (vessel's edge) and nearest compartment bulkhead.

2.   We shall await your reply in due course. Your assistance is appreciated.

G. M. BATES
By direction

Copy to:
BJ, New York (LEG:ADC:aw 61-51-4408-EL (NY 65-104)
BJ, Washington, D.C.

DEPARTMENT OF THE NAVY
OFFICE OF THE JUDGE ADVOCATE GENERAL
WASHINGTON, D.C. 20370

JAG:11:GPS;jat
Ser: 330
1 May 1968

Admiralty and Shipping Section
U.S. Department of Justice
New York, New York 10004
Attn: Mr. A. D. Christian

Re: USS JOSEPH P. KENNEDY, JR.
Visitor's Injury - 3 May 1963 -
Claire D. Dostal v. United States
S.D.N.Y. 65 Ad. 460

Dear Sirs:

We refer to your letter of 9 April 1968 requesting certain information and documents for use in connection with the captioned matter.

We have been unable to locate any of the original injury and consultation reports from the Newport Naval Station Dispensary and Base Hospital. These should have been forwarded to the National Personnel Records Center, St. Louis, Missouri but inquiries directed thereto have proved negative. Commandant, First Naval District and Commander, Cruiser-Destroyer Force, U.S. Atlantic Fleet, have also indicated no knowledge of the whereabouts of these documents. The enclosures evidence that a diligent search has been made for the originals without success. The same enclosure indicates that the missing pages of the plaintiff's statement are also unavailable.

The copy of the enclosed letter from Commanding Officer, U.S., Naval Hospital, Newport, indicates that the original x-rays were forwarded to a private physician in New York and are presumably in the possession of the plaintiff at this time. A copy of the radiographic report is enclosed and we will request the original for possible use at trial.

With regard to the identity of the photographer, we have determined that there are no other means by which we can ascertain his identity.

In accordance with the telephone conversation of 30 April 1968 between Mr. Christian and LT Schwartz we shall await your specific request for a graphic description of the area of the accident.

Sincerely yours,

C. A. BLOCKER
Admiralty Counsel

Copy to:
DJ, Washington, D.C.
CO., JOSEPH P. KENNEDY, JR.

DEPARTMENT OF THE NAVY
OFFICE OF THE JUDGE ADVOCATE GENERAL
WASHINGTON, D.C. 20370

JAG:11:GPS;jat

Ser: 5364
13 June 1968

Admiralty and Shipping Section
U.S. Department of Justice
42 Broadway, Room 600
New York, New York 10004
Attn: Mr. A. D. Christian

               Re: USS JOSEPH P. KENNEDY, JR. - Visitor's
                           Injury - 3 May 1963 - Claire D. Dostal v.
                           United States, S.D.N.Y. 65 Ad. 460
                           Your ref: LXG:ADC:aw 61-51-4408 RL
                           (NY 65-104)

Gentlemen:

Enclosed please find the diagram of the area of the accident as requested in your letter of 1 May 1968.

Sincerely yours,

C. A. BLOCKER
Admiralty Counsel

Copy to:
AdmShppgSec., DJ, Washington

ADMIRALTY AND SHIPPING SECTION
CIVIL DIVISION
DEPARTMENT OF JUSTICE

LEG:REC:gh
61-51-4408
(NY 65-104)

December 4, 1968
Haight, Gardner, Poor & Havens, Esqs.
80 Broad Street
New York, New York 10004

      <u>Attn: Charles S. Haight, Jr., Esq.</u>

      Re: USS JOSEPH P. KENNEDY, JR.
             Visitor's Injury - 3 May 1963
             Claire D. Dostal v. United States
             <u>SDNY   65 Ad. 460</u>

Dear Sirs:

We refer to Mr. Haight's conversation with Mr. Coppola concerning the above case.

Attached please find two separate letters of authorization permitting the Department of Justice to have access to your client's records at both Chamberlayne Junior College in Boston, Mass. And Parsons School of Design here in New York. Kindly have your client sign the original and one copy of each of the attached letters before a notary returning the original and one copy to this office with the third copy for your file.

130

Naturally, any information we obtain from each school will be made available for your perusal. We would appreciate your expediting this matter as trial appears imminent.

Thank you for your cooperation.

Yours very truly,

EDWIN L. WEISL, JR.
Assistant Attorney General
Civil Division

By
Louis E. Greco
Attorney in Charge
Admiralty and Shipping Section

Encs.

LEG:REC:md
61-51-4408
(NY 65-104)

January 10, 1969

Mr. Robert S. Brown
Chamberlayne Junior College
128 Commonwealth Avenue
Boston 16, Massachusetts

> Re: USS JOSEPH P. KENNEDY, JR.
>   Visitor's Injury, May 3, 1963
>   Claire D. Dostal v. United States
>   <u>SDNY   65 Ad. 460</u>

Dear Mr. Brown:

We refer to your conversation with Mr. Coppola concerning the above captioned law suit brought by a former student at Chamberlayne against the United States.

We are in receipt of all the information which you provided as representative of plaintiff's attorneys' corresponding law firm in Boston. As indicated by Mr. Coppola, he would like to meet with you at 11:00 A.M. on Thursday, January 16, 1969, to discuss the circumstances surrounding Miss Dostal's attendance at Chamberlayne and her withdrawal in 1963. We would appreciate your advising Mr. Coppola at (212) 264 0486 if this time proves inconvenient. Our intention is to have your testimony or that of some other knowledgeable individual at Chamberlayn be recorded before a Court

Stenographer for use at the trial in this case in New York. We estimate that this would take not more than one hour and one-half.

We understand that Dean Hassenfus is no longer at Chamberlayne. If our assumption is correct can you provide us with his present address and/or telephone number?

By copy of this letter plaintiff's counsel is being advised of all developments to date and will be present in Boston on the 16th.

Thank you for your cooperation.

Yours very truly,

EDWIN L. WEISL, JR.
Assistant Attorney General
Civil Division

By

Louis E. Greco
Attorney in Charge
Admiralty and Shipping Section

cc: Haight, Gardner, Poor & Havens, Esqs.
         80 Broad Street
         New York, New York 10004

         Attn: Charles S. Haight, Jr., Esq.

ADMIRALTY AND SHIPPING SECTION
CIVIL DIVISION
DEPARTMENT OF JUSTICE

LEG:REC:aw
61-51-4408
(NY 67-104)

January 15, 1969

<u>BY</u> <u>HAND</u>

Parsons School of Design
410 East 54th Street
New York, N.Y.

Attention: Miss Abernathy
<u>Registrar</u>

        Re: USS JOSEPH P. KENNEDY, JR.
               Visitor's Injury, May 3, 1963
               Claire D. Dostal, et al. v. United States
               <u> SDNY   65 Ad. 460   </u>

Dear Sirs:

We refer to Mr. Coppola's conversation with Miss Abernathy concerning the above case brought by a former student of yours against the government for injuries allegedly sustained aboard an U.S. Navy destroyer in May, 1963.

Plaintiff Claire Dostal, was a student at Parsons School of Design in 1964 or 1965.

134

Would you kindly provide thermofax or xerox copies of the following documents and affix the seal of Parsons School to each of them:

Any application prepared by Miss Dostal requesting admittance to Parsons; a transcript of her scholastic record; the medical certificate or report submitted on entering Parsons; attendance records for the entire period of time Miss Dostal was enrolled at Parsons.

We would also appreciate any other information pertaining to Miss Dostal which may be contained in any other files maintained by your office. Specifically, should absences from class require medical substantiation, we would appreciate copies of anything submitted by Miss Dostal in this regard.

If you have any question, please call Mr. Coppola at 264-0486.

We thank Miss Abernathy for her cooperation.

Very truly yours,

EDWIN L. WEISL, JR.
Assistant Attorney General
Civil Division

By

Louis E. Greco
Attorney in Charge
Admiralty and Shipping Section

FACTS AND DISCUSSION

Plaintiff Claire Dostal, an eighteen year old unmarried female, was injured on May 3, 1963 when she fell into the water from the deck of USS JOSEPH P. KENNEDY, a Public vessel of the United States.

Plaintiff and a girl friend went aboard KENNEDY at Newport, Rhode Island, to visit a crewmember. While on the main deck conversing with her friends, a restraining lifeline gave way and plaintiff fell, back first, over the port side of KENNEDY striking her back on the hull of a vessel nested alongside before entering into the water. Plaintiff remained in the water approximately six minutes until she was rescued by KENNEDY crew members.

The protective lifeline which gave way was one that had recently been separated to allow the placing of a brow between KENNEDY and the adjoining vessel. The unsecured end was merely doubled back and rested on a hook located on a stanchion. As a result of the Navy investigation, it was recommended that loose lifelines be wrapped around the stanchion prior to being placed on the hooks.

Plaintiff testified at her discovery deposition that she merely placed her elbow on the lifeline and it gave way. There was a question whether the plaintiff exerted her full weight against the lifeline or just rested an elbow on it. The witnesses testified that the latter occurred. In any event, there was no warning against such usage of the restraining barrier. There is no evidence that plaintiff was negligent in any manner. <u>D'Amico v. United States</u>, 62 Ad. 1180, S.D.N.Y., November 27, 1964; aff'd., Docket #29882, 2d. Cir., March 3, 1966 (unreported). Although plaintiff was not entitled to a warranty of seaworthiness the Navy did owe her the duty of

136

reasonable care. <u>Kermarec v. Compaignie Generale Transatlantique</u>, 358 U. S. 625 (1959). The United states did not meet this duty.

Immediately following the accident, Miss Dostal was given emergency treatment aboard the vessel and then taken to the United States Naval hospital at Newport. X-rays taken there were negative and Miss Dostal was released.

She then went to a private doctor in Boston where she attended college. He and other treating doctors were of the opinion she suffered a fractured coccyx.

Our doctors claim the coccyx was not fractured, but that what appears on some x-rays to indicate a fracture was really a shadow caused by her doctors' position of the trauma area at the time the films were taken. Miss Dostal was examined on the Government's behalf by an orthopedist, gynecologist and radiologist. While our doctors agreed she suffered no fracture, they also agreed that whether or not the coccyx was fractured, Miss Dostal had and would suffer pain.

In addition, plaintiff claims that as a result of this injury, she still suffers from irregular and painful menses. While our gynecologist says she will experience no difficulty with respect to reproduction., he found it difficult to state categorically that these symptoms could not be related to the accident.

At the time of her accident, plaintiff was a first year student at a junior college in Boston. Allegedly, as a result of this accident, plaintiff missed the remainder of her classes (from May 5) causing her to fail her final exams in June. Consequently, she was dismissed from school with no credit for that semester. Her father and mother claimed approximately $1,400 for lost tuition and related expenses.

The amount was confirmed and the only question was whether the accident was the proximate cause other than dismissal from school. Records of the school indicate that plaintiff may have missed classes for a variety of reasons prior to her accident aboard KENNEDY. Certain records pertaining to the exact number of absences both before and after May 3, 1965 were destroyed by the school. Interviews with school officials disclosed, at the very least, her dismissal was related to the absences after the accident. Whether (and to what extent) prior conduct contributed is unknown.

There is no question that she was under a doctor's care in Boston during May and June. After dismissal, plaintiff made appropriate attempts to be readmitted, but all were denied. The school specifically stated they considered the accident as excusing the absences, but denied readmission on the basis that relief should have been requested before final exams. Plaintiff's first semester grades were excellent.

She later continued her education in the same field at another school, graduating in 1968. She received no transfer credit for any work in the second semester at the junior college and only minimal credit for the first semesters work where she compiled an outstanding academic record.

Without doubt, we would be held liable for the loss of a major part of the college expenses, and, in all probability, the whole amount, considering the KENNEDY accident as the proximate cause of her absences and subsequent dismissal.

In addition, plaintiff claims the sum of $268.52 for personal effects when her purse sank after her fall. This loss was confirmed by the Navy. Plaintiff's medical bills and expenses came to about $1,000.00; thus, her total "specials" are approximately $2,700.00.

The case was called for a pre-trial conference, where, after hearing both sides, Judge Walter R. Mansfield reasoned that a "fair, but parsimonious" settlement figure would be $15 000.00. The Court unequivocably stated that a judgment after trial would be for a far greater sum. The pre-trial judge stated that the Government had no defense and it was simply a question of how much plaintiff would recover. With this, we are constrained to agree.

We are faced with a pretty, young plaintiff, who, because of our negligence, fell from the deck of a ship into the water after striking her back against an adjoining vessel. An award for pain and suffering would also consider her having remained in the water for about six minutes before rescue.

Plaintiff alleges serious injuries with concomitant "mental" complaints affecting her personality. This mild form of conversion hysteria is reflected in her statements about doubts as to her reproductive capabilities when, and if, she were to marry. There is no doubt that the injury in this case, to a very.sensitive area of the body, could produce the "mental" suffering complained of by plaintiff. This condition, coincident to, and the natural result of her physical injury, is recoverable in damages. <u>Leatherman v. Gateway Transportation Co.</u>, 331 F.2d 241 (7th Cir 1964). While plaintiff's claim for continued pain and menstrual difficulties is less clear as to extent, it cannot be disproven or even seriously questioned.

After several months of negotiations, counsel for plaintiff advised that his clients would reluctantly agree to offer to settle for $15,000. Counsel strongly recommended this figure as expenses for plaintiff's medical experts would be considerable in this case. We rejected the offer and arrangements were made to go to Boston for the taking of the deposition de bene esse of one of plaintiff's doctors and officials at the junior college.

The day before the scheduled depositions in Boston, this case came on for a final settlement conference before Judge Sylvester J. Ryan. At this conference., counsel for plaintiff indicated the willingness of his clients to accept $13,500.00. We agreed to recommend acceptance of this offer.

There is no doubt that should this case proceed to trial, plaintiff would recover a greater sum. Of lesser importance, but obviously relevant, would be the costs of the deposition in Boston and the fees for experts on the Government's behalf. There is no doubt that settlement on these terms is most advantageous to the Government.

On January 16, 1969, the facts and circumstances of this case were discussed with the Department of the Navy. By letter dated January 28, 1969, the Department of the Navy, expressed their concurrence in our recommendation to accept the offer in compromise.

<u>CONCLUSION</u>

By reason for the foregoing, I recommend that the offer in compromise whereby plaintiffs will recover $13,500.00, without interest and without costs, be accepted.

Louis E. Greco
Attorney in Charge
New York Office